2-20-16

MW01489916

Hope this gives you something to add to your writings.

Best Wishes,

CHALLENGING CHOICES

●

WELCOME LIFE'S INVITATIONS
TO INCREASE YOUR VISION

By Cliff Bennett

ISBN: 1453647244
ISBN-13: 9781453647240

Table of Contents

The secret of contentment is the discovery by every man of his own powers and limitations, finding satisfaction in a line of activity which he can do well, plus the wisdom to know that his place, no matter how important or successful he is, never count very much in the universe. A man may very well be so successful in carving a name for himself in his field that he begins to imagine himself indispensable or omnipotent. He is eaten up be some secret ambition, and then good-bye to all contentment. Sometimes it is more important to discover what one cannot do than what one can do. So much restlessness is due to the fact that a man does not know what he wants, or he wants too many things, or perhaps he wants to be somebody else. To be anybody except himself.

The courage of being one's genuine self, of standing alone and of not wanting to be somebody else.

- Lin Yutang
Chinese writer and inventor

Foreword

The acorn becomes an oak by means of automatic growth; no commitment is necessary. The kitten similarly becomes a cat on the basis of instinct. Nature and being are identical in creatures like them. But a man or woman becomes fully human only by his or her choices and his or her commitment to them. People attain worth and dignity by the multitude of decisions they make from day by day. These decisions require courage.

- Rollo May, MD
Psychiatrist, psychotherapist, and author

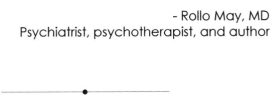

It is the whole process of meeting and solving problems that life has meaning. Problems are the cutting edge that distinguishes between success and failure. Problems call forth our courage and our wisdom; indeed they create our courage and our wisdom. It is only because of problems that we grow mentally and spiritually. It is through the pain of confronting and resolving problems that we learn.

- M. Scott Peck, M.D.
American psychiatrist and prolific author

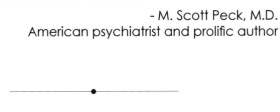

However mean your life is, meet it and live it; do not shun and call it names. It is not so bad as you are. It looks poorest when you are richest. The fault-finder will find faults in paradise. Love your life.

- Henry David Thoreau
American philosopher and author

All that we are is the result of what we have thought. The mind is everything. What we think, we become.

- Buddha

Sixty years ago I knew everything; now I know nothing. Education is the progressive study of our own ignorance.

- Will Durant

WHAT IS IMPORTANT is to keep learning, to enjoy challenge, and to tolerate ambiguity. In the end there are no certain answers.

- Martina Horner
President, Radcliffe College

Ours is an excessively conscious age. We know so much, we feel so little.

–D.H. Lawrence

Acknowledgments

This book expresses my gratitude to all surrogate parents, friends, teachers, coaches, professors, colleagues, and students, for being my support system.

I am beholden to all the authors for their profound insight, wisdom, and depth inspiring quotes that I've included. They provide definitive meaning that enhance the purpose of this book.

To my children, Brian, Cindy, Susan, and Bruce, thanks for your forgiveness, understanding, and especially eight wonderful grandchildren. Thanks for the joy and pride you give me. I love you all.

Special thanks to my son Brian for being the catalyst that enabled me to finish this work. Your twenty-first-century knowledge and competence is amazing. Thanks, B, for your encouragement and advice.

To Judy, my best friend and wife, I give you special thanks for your respect and love. With you, I survived and found balance. Thanks for being you and for your patience, understanding, and assistance with the lengthy process of finalizing all the drafts to complete this book. I love you.

To the professional staff of CreateSpace.com, I commend all of you for your expert help in finalizing this project.

Keep constantly in mind how many things you yourself have witnessed changes already. The universe is change, life is understanding.

- Marcus Aurelis

Time is the coin of your life. It is the only coin you have, and only you can determine how it will be spent. Be careful lest you let other people spend it for you.

- Carl Sandberg

If your daily life seems poor, do not blame it; blame yourself. Tell yourself that you are not poet enough to call forth its riches.

- Rainer Maria Rilke

Mans highest merit always is, as much as much as possible, to rule external circumstances and as little as possible to let himself be ruled by them.

- Goethe

Preface

Life is a song, sing it.
Life is a game, play it.
Life is challenge meet it
Life is a dream, realize it.
Life is a sacrifice, offer it.
Life is love, enjoy it.

- Sai Baba
Popular South Indian guru, spiritual figure, and educator

When you are inspired by some great purpose, some extraordinary project, all your thoughts break their bonds; your mind transcends limitations, your consciousness expands in every direction, And you find yourself in a new, great and wonderful world. Dormant forces, faculties and talents become alive, and you discover yourself to be a greater person by far than you ever dreamed yourself to be.

- Patanjali

The author of Yoga Sutras, Patanjali lived in India.

The truth that many people never understand, until it is too late, is that the more you try to avoid suffering, the more you suffer, because smaller and more insignificant things begin to torture you in proportion to your fear of being hurt.

- Thomas Merton

What lies behind us and what lies before us are tiny matters, compared to what lies within us.

- Oliver Wendell Holmes

Be of good courage all is before you, and time passed in the difficult is nerve lost...what is required of us is that we love the difficult and learn to deal with it. In the difficult are the friendly forces, the hands that work on us.

- Rainer Maria Rilke

Make it a rule of life never to regret and never to look back. Regret is an appalling waste of energy: you can't build on it; it only good for wallowing in.

- Katherine Mansfield

Words are of course, the most powerful drugs used by mankind.

-Rudyard Kipling

Introduction

Start doing what's necessary, then what's possible, and suddenly you are doing the impossible.

- St. Francis of Assisi

Life is not about finding yourself.
Life is about creating yourself.

-Anonymous

CHALLENGING CHOICES – Welcome Life's Invitations To Increase Your Vision is a trilogy in one book, the common mission of the three sections, **Memoir, Holistic Prescriptions for Continuous Personal Growth** and **Empowering Poems** is to get the most from experiencing life. Together, they interpret the need to live with courage, purpose, commitment, and accomplishment by drawing on the power we all have within the human spirit, to become a winning trifecta ticket.

The first section is the vivid real life, anecdotally rich story of my personal experiences and an inside view of my forty-two year career as a teacher and administrator in public and higher education. Changes in our way of life, past and present, are explored by contrasting differences in American Society and culture over the last sixty years.

Summarizing and synthesizing knowledge and skills I learned serving as Director of Student Services and Health Education, is a how to section on practicing proactive positive self-power. Holistic prescriptions for continuous personal growth to help you embrace personal responsibilities for managing and maintaining a state of wellness – caring enough for yourself, so you care for yourself. By applying these skills, we empower and enhance our lives through self-discipline and practicing preventive, positive health habits.

Augmenting these two aspects of self-growth is a section of poetic verse that reflects my reactions to life. They coalesce the emotions being expressed internally in my heart, mind, and soul. A meaningful poem distills feelings that empowers the reader to capture the depth felt by the poet. Like wine transforming into cognac.

These three dimensions connect in harmony, to create the desire and determination to fulfill our heart's song, to fight against negative intrusions, pessimism, and apathy. To live a life accepting challenges, making choices that achieve our life's purpose. To invite life's trials to strengthen our character and perseverance. To value life and our lives. To look for and find silver linings. To solve life's problems. To count and appreciate our blessings. To laugh and smile more. To pursue happiness. To maintain a positive attitude.

- Cliff Bennett

———————————•———————————

This is perhaps the most beautiful time in human history; it is really pregnant with all kinds of creative possibilities made possible by science and technology which now constitute the slave of man – if man is not enslaved by it.

-Jonas Salk MD

———————————•———————————

Problems are only opportunities in work clothes.

- Henry J. Kaiser

———————————•———————————

I shall tell you a great secret, my friend. Do not wait for the last judgment; it takes place every day.

- Albert Camus

Living through World War II

At Home: Early Memories
1940 – 1950

It isn't always others who enslave us. Sometimes we let circumstances enslave us, sometimes we let things enslave us, [and] sometimes, with weak wills, we enslave ourselves.

- Richard L. Evans

Loneliness and the feeling of being unwanted are the most terrible poverty.

–Mother Teresa

Adversity in the things of this world opens the door for spiritual salvation.

-Arnold J. Toynbee

The first year I remember is 1940. I was living with my family in an odious third-floor, walk-up apartment on Main Street, in Mineola, New York, 100 feet from the railroad tracks and train station. If God decided Long Island needed an enema, he would stick the nozzle there.

Although I was young, I hated my given name, Clifford, especially being a *junior* (because my father was also Clifford Bennett). My mother picked up on this and nicknamed me Buddy, which stayed with me through high school. Those early memories were not pleasant ones. Here's why.

When I was born on May 21, 1936, my mother (May) was thirty years old and my father was fifty-two. Not only was the age difference significant, he was also obese, sickly, and seldom worked. Our family was living on public assistance as a result of my father losing all of his investments in the 1929 stock market crash. Up until then, my parents and two older sisters, Gloria and Phoebe, lived in a comfortable brick house in East Williston and were living a good middle class life on stock dividends. The crash, according to my mom, had devastated my father who remained depressed, lonely, and passive for the rest of his life. He was either in a chair or on the couch, usually smoking a cigar, and seldom spoke. If you asked him a question, you got a one or two-word answer, at best.

The apartment we lived in was above a kosher chicken market. The chickens would graze and feed in the open space behind the store. I remember the Afro-American man who would take me with him on occasion in the delivery truck. I was in awe at his energy, enthusiasm, and joyous attitude toward life. He was happy. I had never experienced that before. I think his name was Jim. He taught me how to whistle and even tried to show me how to tap dance. How I loved to be with him! He was my first of many positive role models and surrogate fathers.

On one Sunday evening, after supper, I vividly remember how my mother, sisters, and I were noticing smoke and hundreds of cockroaches coming up into the living room and kitchen area from the baseboards. The odor was causing us to get nauseous. We thought the building was on fire and helped my father down the two flights of stairs to the street. My mother went to the corner stationery store and had them call the fire department. The firemen went into both apartments to find the fire. What they found was the male tenant who lived underneath us sitting in his kitchen wearing a gas mask! He had decided to light pesticide gas canisters and fumigate his apartment for the infestation of cockroaches. He never thought this would be a problem since he was wearing a gas mask! After extinguishing and removing the canisters, as well as a period of ventilating both apartments, we were permitted to return. Although I was only five, I couldn't believe his stupidity (it also didn't help with the constant cockroach problem).

My mother was a devout Lutheran and always sang in the church choir. She had a strong, loud voice like Ethel Merman. The Lutheran church we went to had a school across the street, (behind the Jewish synagogue), which I attended. (I never could figure out how my mother could afford to send me there.) Social Services had brought me a new pair of shoes since I had out grown the old ones. I was around eight years old when my mother presented me with my new shoes—girl's black patent leather, strapped shoes (I think they are called Mary Janes). No way was I going to school wearing girl's shoes! Surely there's been a mistake... perhaps they were brought for my sisters! No, my mother insisted I had to wear them, which, of course, I did. As I walked closer to the schoolyard and saw some students playing, I knew I couldn't face them wearing those horrid shoes. So I got down on one knee and using the sand and gravel from the schoolyard, I rubbed off the black patent leather from both shoes (it came off rather easily). I felt the shoes, and even though the strap was still there, didn't look too bad; so I ventured forth, and much to my surprise, no classmate mocked or made fun of me. I'll never forget the feeling of embarrassment I experienced from that incident. My mother noticed the dull brown shoes I came home with, and I soon had a new pair of sneakers to wear. Sneakers were much cheaper than shoes then.

Looking back on my early childhood with it's periods of knowing I didn't have much stuff and what we had at home was different from what others kids had, an article I read recently in an educational research journal sure made sense. The article addressed the issue of how poor children, or children who have poor role models for parents, still come out of that environment able to succeed in school and life. Seems that if a parent(s) or teacher(s) (as surrogate parents) remembers and celebrates the child's birthday and significant holidays that this is enough for the child to feel okay. Just the anticipation that these special occasions will happen, makes the child feel special (albeit for an hour or two). They are enough to compensate for all the other times of emptiness and loneliness. Having been there and done that,

I can validate how important those magical moments are and how they gave me hope for the future. I also remember my older sister criticizing my mother for spending too much money one Christmas, so that sent a mixed message, discounted the gifts, and prompted feelings of guilt. Somehow though, it was enough to keep you going and tolerating your day-to-day bare existence.

During the summer of 1942, we moved to Williston Park, about five miles north of Mineola. My father's health was better, and he was working a day shift at Grumman Aircraft, along with my mother and sister Gloria who worked two different shifts. Grumman ran round the clock, making planes for our aircraft carriers during World War II. My sister Phoebe had a job with the Long Island Lighting Company as a clerk. Because money was coming in, we were able to rent a house on Syracuse Street, and I entered the Mineola public school system at the Cross Street Elementary School.

Life then literally revolved around the war. The media and movies scripted you to hate the Japs and the Nazis. The war supplies engine drove the economy. Meat, butter, tires, batteries, and other items were rationed. To purchase any of these commodities, you needed the prescribed number of red tokens, in addition to the cash. It seemed that every other house had a star or two hanging in the window, indicating a member(s) of that family was serving in one of the armed forces. Headlights on all cars had to have the top half painted black to prevent the light from being seen from the sky. I never could understand that. Each block had an air raid drill leader who had a special helmet and insignia. I remember how everyone celebrated V-J and V-E Days by dancing in the streets, blowing horns, and banging pots. To this day, from the imprints of WW II, especially the negative impression of the Japanese, I still have a hard time being open to their culture and cannot bring myself to buy a Japanese car, no matter how good they are. That's how strong the imprints were and are.

This societal conditioning showed later in high school and my years working as an educator. Stereotypes and prejudice were also strong when it came to blacks, other minority groups, and especially different religions (any other than yours).

I experienced fear and anxiety from some teachers when dealing with disadvantaged people who were different from them. Cultural and religious biases were frequent issues I had to include in problem solving human relations issues. And, the dynamic worked both ways. This social gravity affected everyone. More about this later.

In 1945, because of the steady employment Grumman provided my family, my mother and father purchased a house in Williston Park, just four blocks south on Harvard Street for $3,800.00. I stayed in the same elementary school. My father became sickly again and stopped working. Grumman laid off my mother, and finances became tight again. Both of my sisters worked and contributed to pay for household expenses. Around the age of twelve, I began caddying and was expected to turn over at least half of what I made to my mother. I accepted this as normal, although none of my friends had to do this.

I'll never forget two incidents that occurred while I was a student at the Cross Street Elementary School. The first was when I was a fifth grader. The teacher, I forgot (probably repressed) her name, told us the fifth grade classes were presenting at the next P.T.A. meeting. Since we were studying the planets, our class would put on a presentation about the order of the planets from the sun. To do this, the nine of us chosen were to get a shoebox, label the front with the name of the planet we were representing (I was Pluto), cut a hole in the front and back, so we could put a flashlight in the box and light it on command from our teacher. Oh, how I remember the grief I got asking for a shoebox and to have to purchase a flashlight! Somehow, I was given my planetary necessities.

The evening of the P.T.A. presentation, the nine students were waiting backstage with our teacher for our moment of astronomical fame. I remember the teacher telling us how to line up so when the curtains were opened, we would be in perfect order, from the sun. When she called out our planets name, we were to put on our flashlight to show our relative position to the sun. I was told to go off the stage, out the stage door, and stand in the corridor, since Pluto was the furthest out. My classmate "Neptune" was also off stage left but not out in the corridor. As I nervously waited for my teacher to call out "Pluto," a custodian who was dragging the corridor floor wanted to know why I was out in the hallway and told me to get back on the stage, where I belonged; just then I finally heard "and now Pluto." I couldn't believe between the grief I received from my parents (for having to get a shoebox and buy a flashlight) and the custodian, in my few seconds of planethood glory, that no one could see my flashlight, box or me because Neptune and Pluto couldn't be seen from the audience! Only the teacher could see us.

The other incident was ego crushing and self-esteem draining. Ms. Hughes, our sixth grade teacher, while studying a play, made a big deal out of explaining what *typecasting* meant. Since we were going to put on our class play for the P.T.A., each student was going to be given a part that best suited his or her looks and personality. I was chosen to be "lard pail," a fifteen-year-old fatty. Bad enough I had to go back on that dreaded stage again, but as *Lard Pail* in front of all my classmates? No way! However, I survived the experience, but my mother wasn't pleased.

The areas around Williston Park were still semi-rural in the early '50s so there were many opportunities to have fun and enjoy the environment. My buddy Bob Wittemann and I spent many an hour fishing in local ponds for carp and goldfish. Our "tackle" consisted of a straight, light five- or six-foot tree branch with about ten feet of number eight black thread at the end tied to a bent straight pin. You would attach whatever wood you could find on the ground as a "bobber," wrap a compressed wet piece of bread on the pin "hook", and wait for bites, which were often. We never caught anything big but always had action; especially when we could afford to buy some cheesecloth, which, with a handful of oatmeal in the middle, made great chum.

Bob and I decided to make a raft that we could use to fish from, instead of always standing on the branches of a fallen tree, which protruded out into Perks Pond. Somehow we salvaged enough lumber from discarded pallets and nailed together about an eight-foot long by seven-foot wide raft. We spent our allowances and savings on lead putty, which we put in all the cracks, hoping to make our raft seaworthy.

Finally came the day, we were ready to float our craft. Using two wagons, we managed to get the raft to the side of Perks Pond. I was worried the raft was too heavy and wouldn't float. Bobby assured me not to worry. I was right! I'll never forget slowly pushing the raft into the pond and then the raft never rising in the water. It just hugged the bottom of the pond basin and sank. I think we both laughed and cried as we saw the raft remain submerged. So much for raft and boatbuilding! My first lesson in physics—buoyancy dynamics.

Once we turned fourteen, our outdoor interests turned to hunting and trapping. There were large fields, woods, and streams west and north of Williston Park, where we could hunt squirrels, rabbits, and pheasants. During the fall we would set six to twelve traps for muskrats in the streams. We would take turns checking and baiting the traps every other day. Believe it or not, we would catch a muskrat every so often, skin it, and send the pelt, (salted), to Sears Roebuck in Chicago. We were thrilled when we'd get a check for between $2.75 and $3.50 for each pelt, depending on the condition and quality of the fur. We had a lot of fun, and I learned to love the outdoors. To this day, I would much rather be outside, than in. When I'm close to nature, I'm close to God.

Bob Wittemann was two years older than me (he was around fourteen at this time), suggested I try caddying, which he had been doing. He taught me how to tend the flag (pin) on the green, the purpose of the different clubs, and the basic rules and tips a caddy should know. I felt pretty confident with all his schooling. So one Sunday morning, he told me to make a bag lunch and go with him to the Garden City Golf Club to get a "loop". Although I was afraid I looked too young (you were supposed to be fourteen to qualify for caddying), I was big for my age, and coupled with Bobby's training, I felt sure caddying would be easy. Was I wrong!

Around 2:00 P.M. in the afternoon, with no other caddies left in the caddy yard, I decided it was time to eat my sandwich and go home by myself since it was obvious I was not going to get a "loop". Just as I was getting up to leave, the caddy master looked out the window and called me over to him.

"How old are you?" he asked.

"Fourteen," I lied.

"Ever caddy before?"

"Yes," I replied hoping that was the end of the questions. It was.

"I have a brand new member who just wants to play nine holes. Treat him good. Go around front, and I'll give you his bag. He's waiting at the first tee."

"Okay. Thanks," I replied.

The first mistake I made, as I was approaching the first tee, was carrying his bag backwards (the clubs were facing my back). My golfer, a man about forty, wearing glasses and new golf attire, let me know I was carrying the bag backward. Although embarrassed, that was easy to correct, so despite a bad start, I managed to follow Bob's directions well for the first three holes. Things were going smoothly until my golfer's approach shot on the fourth hole. He had hit a very high nine iron into the bunker on the right side of the green. The ball "plugged" into the steep embankment and was going to be tough to get airborne and out of the sand. He walked into the sand trap, dug his feet in, and asked me for "dynamite." At least that's what I thought he said. Actually, he had asked for his "dynamiter," which was the name of a Spalding sand wedge. Bob never told me about a dynamiter. Sand wedge—yes, but not a dynamiter. My naïve inexperienced mind had looked at his buried ball, the height of the green, and assumed he was going to use a small stick of dynamite to blow the ball up on to the green.

So, upon hearing him ask for dynamite (I never heard the R), I started to zip open the side of his bag to get him the small piece of dynamite. Although his back was toward me, he could hear the zipper opening.

He turned and very angrily asked, "What the hell are you doing going into my bag?"

I replied, "To get you the dynamite you asked for."

"I didn't ask for dynamite, you asshole. I asked for my dynamiter, my sand wedge!"

Talk about embarrassing moments! I tried to apologize and handed him his dynamiter. Mumbling under his breath, he managed to hit a great shot out of the trap, the ball landing close to the pin. I gave him his putter, took out the pin, and he made the putt. But he was still very upset with me. So upset, he said I ruined his concentration and was cutting back across the course to play the eighteenth hole and quitting because I had ruined his round of golf!

The eighteenth hole at the Garden City Country Club is about 150 yards straight over a pond. The eighteenth green is situated so the clubhouse-restaurant is built L shaped facing the green so persons inside can watch the players putt out. My friend Bobby had told me if the player hits close to the pin, give him the putter, go before him, take the pin out, and stand to the side. This would speed things up. My golfer hit a great shot, probably <u>eight feet</u> from the pin. So this was my big opportunity to make up for my blunder at the last hole!

I walked up to my still angry golfer, congratulated him on a great shot, gave him his putter, and proceeded in front of him at a fast clip to get the pin out. It was obvious to me the cup was close to his ball. As I walked over to the side of the green, I couldn't help but notice the number of people sitting inside the clubhouse watching out the windows. Now my golfer has arrived, and is getting ready to putt. However, even though I can see the cup near him and the ball, he doesn't. And here I am standing with the pin upright <u>on top of my right shoe!</u> I couldn't understand why he was lining his putt up on my right foot. I assumed he was going to take a practice putt! Now, here comes the ball, straight and at a perfect speed it gently bounces off the front of my right shoe. It would have been a perfect fifty-foot putt, except the cup isn't there.

He looks at me and says, "Why the hell didn't you take the pin out of the hole?"

"Because this isn't the hole," I answered, pointing to the hole. "It's right in front of you by your right shoulder. I thought you knew that but decided to take a practice putt."

With that inadequate explanation, he took his putter, threw it up into the air, started swearing, and called me the worst caddy in the United States. The caddy master must have heard the laughter from the clubhouse lounge area and came out to rescue me.

"Here is thirty-five cents, son. It's the minimum caddy fee for five holes. Take it and never come back to this course."

After that experience, I wasn't sure I would ever try caddying again. But after a few weeks, I went with Bob to the Wheatley Hills Golf Club in East Williston, and had no problems. I caddied there for many years. Now that I play golf, I cannot imagine getting so upset at a very young caddy while playing a practice round by myself. Other golfers sure get a kick out of that anecdote. I hope you did, too. I didn't at the time. But now I can look back at it and laugh.

Around the time I was twelve, I remember Bob and many other neighborhood kids played and hung out in a large vacant house off Willis Avenue. The side door to the house was open and although there was some furniture in it, what was left was in very bad shape. It was abandoned. One time when Bob, Roger, and I went to play in the house, I saw a small hole in the kitchen floor that was apparently caused by a fire. We didn't pay any attention to it. However, about a week after our last visit to the house, Nassau County detectives showed up at the Cross Street Elementary School wanting to talk to Roger and me about the fire in the house. We were accused of breaking and entering (which wasn't true), and setting the fire (which also wasn't true). We tried to tell the detectives that just about everyone in the neighborhood played in it and that it was known to be open and a hangout.

We were brought up on juvenile delinquency charges and had to go to court. Apparently well-connected, wealthy Republicans who wanted a scapegoat owned the house. We were it. I'll never forget being so nervous and embarrassed. My mother and father had to come to court because of me. For some reason, while I thought I was crying, the judge perceived I was laughing and reprimanded me for thinking my actions were not serious. Nothing could have been further from the truth! Since the owners of the house wanted justice, even though there was no proof we forcibly entered the house and set the fire, we were found guilty. The judge suspended our sentence since we did not have a previous record and lectured our parents to correct our errant ways. We were placed on probation for a year. I'll never forget being called a juvenile delinquent and learning what it meant to be from on the wrong side of the socioeconomic tracks (Williston Park) instead of East Williston.

The Mineola Schools were organized in the late '40s so that seventh grade was part of the elementary school. A school in Mineola that was converted during the war to a training facility to produce labor for the war effort was converted back to a public school, and the year I went there (1949-1950), it just housed the eighth grade. One of the courses we took was mechanical drawing. Our teacher, a woman, was the most terrifying teacher I ever experienced. I forget her real name, but her student-given nickname was Zelda, Queen of the Jungle. Once, when I was drawing, she came by my desk and obviously didn't like what I had tried to draw. I was instructed to make a fist, hold my knuckles still, so she could whack them with a triangular drawing ruler. I still remember seeing stars when she hit my knuckles and the blood dripping on my drawing. That's one way to get you to start over! To this day, I hate mechanical drawing and dreaded having to take engineering drawing in college!

During my early adolescent years, I became more aware of the poor role model my father was. Now that I was thirteen, he was sixty-three, an old, lazy sixty-three. He hadn't worked in years and usually just sat and watched TV.

I know little of my father's experiences and worldview. What I did know was that he was the youngest of thirteen children, born and raised on a truck farm in Brooklyn. He never spoke of his family, and I never met any of my aunts or uncles. *Strange.* According to my mother (my father practically never spoke), he only received a formal education through the sixth grade. He was very good at arithmetic, able to add and subtract large numbers in his head. That's the only skill I knew he had, and it helped him get some work in the insurance industry as an auditor.

He, his upbringing, family, interests, goals, disappointments, etc. remain a mystery. All I knew was he was my father and still lived with my mother. To my knowledge, he never initiated a conversation with me, my mother, or sisters. Although I do remember him chastising my sisters and me if we went to the bathroom immediately upon entering the house with "you should have used somebody else's water! Do you know it take four gallons to flush a toilet?" Another favorite was "Never stand when you can sit, and never sit when you can lie." He was like a boarder in a rooming house. *Weird.*

My only positive memory was when he took me to Yankee stadium in the Bronx to see the Yanks play the Red Sox. I was so excited to go on the bus and then the subway. I remember our seats were pretty high up, but we had a good view from near the first base side. I couldn't believe my eyes when Ted Williams, playing left field for the Red Sox, dropped an easy pop fly, he trotted in to catch. The New York fans got on his case, and he responded by giving the "Italian salute" several times to the fans. I lost a lot of respect I held for professional athletes with those arm gestures. I thought Ted Williams (or any professional athlete) should have more class and not lower himself to such bush-league behavior. Now look at Dennis Rodman, Mike Tyson, and other million-dollar babies.

For several months in 1949-1950, my father obviously had a tumor growing in the right front edge of his tongue. You could see it inside his mouth and as the months went by, it grew so large it protruded from his mouth. Of course, all during this time, my mother, sisters, and I pleaded with him to go to a dentist or physician to get treatment. My father dreaded any kind of medical doctor and refused to go. Finally, with the tumor so big he couldn't close his lips, he agreed to go to a dentist, who immediately referred him to the Cancer Clinic at Meadowbrook Hospital, now the Nassau County Medical Center. Most of his tongue had to be removed. Cancer treatments then were primitive. About two months after the surgery, they found cancer cells in the lymph nodes in his neck, which they removed. So now, in addition to not having a tongue, his neck was deformed. Once a week for about two months, he had to go for radiation therapy, which was new at that time. I remember how his face and neck would be burned from the radiation. Through this tough treatment, they were able to arrest the cancer. Because the cancer was caused by smoking cigars, I have an aversion to cigar smoke to this day. I actually get nauseous when I smell it or see someone smoking a cigar.

Given the age gap between my mother and father, and his failing health, not working, and being depressed and silent, it wasn't a surprise when my mother announced to my sisters and I that she was getting legally separated from him. This was at the end of my seventh grade school year. Although we all knew there was no relationship between them (I never remember them sleeping together, hugging, or displaying any sign of affection), what puzzled us (especially me), was that she agreed to let him stay in the house, sleeping in the same separate room he always had. Although I guess my mother had her reasons and felt it necessary to do this, it was a very awkward situation.

They never went to the movies or out to dinner. There wasn't even any conversation back and forth between them at the supper table, other than "pass the salt or pepper." This distorted my perception of marriage. I was living in a very atypical situation. Perhaps my mother and father, because of their age difference, switched roles. She became his mother and he, her son?

I also found out from my sister Phoebe recently that back in the mid-1930s, my mother wanted to have another child, a boy. Even then they were "separated" and according to Phoebe, my mother had to "seduce" him to produce me. Not very comforting news, and too much information.

Things were so tense in the house now, that I tried as hard as I could to be there as little as possible. Any new friend thought because of my father's age, physical problems, and lethargy, that he was my grandfather. I hated trying to defend-explain that he was my father. As a consequence, I valued the time I spent in my friends' homes. It was a pleasure to actually see wife and husband communicate and show affection to each other. My friends' fathers also went fishing, hunting, and took care of their house and property.

To this day, I am grateful to my friend's parents for being the role models I so desperately needed. Looking back, my surrogate parents in a sense had adopted me as a result of me adopting them. That was my first challenging choice. Getting a glimpse of normality was important to me being in a home dominated by a strong mother (although caring) and two sisters. I had a father, but I never knew a dad.

Searching for a Support System

Finding Surrogate Parents
Surviving Adolescence
High School culture
1950-1954

Lifeguard at Bar Beach 1956.

All men should strive to learn before they die, what they are running from, and to, and why.

- James Thurber

Those things that hurt, instruct.

- Benjamin Franklin

———————————•———————————

I was glad to start high school because of the opportunities to play sports. High school in the early 1950's was structured around the importance of dating, being popular, and playing sports. Thank God I was interested in playing baseball (later lacrosse), and football. Although not good enough to make the school basketball team, I played basketball throughout high school for our Lutheran church team. Neither of my parents went beyond the sixth grade, which was common then, so they didn't push me to think about a career or going to college. Easily influenced by my neighborhood buddies and peers, I followed my two best friends who were taking all the easiest courses and going into auto shop for their high school major sequence. There was great pressure to do what was popular and the peer *in thing*. The student body consisted of the jocks, nerds, hoods, and the white-buck-shoed academics. You could survive if you did things that cut across group lines, like play sports or were popular for some other reason, like being a class leader.

Stereotyping was rampant, as was pigeonholing and scapegoat hunting. Mineola High School was a microcosm of American society, the macrocosm at the time for prejudice and fear. No matter what your ethnic background, you were stereotyped. If you were Irish, you were a "Mick"; if Italian, a "Guinea"; Polish, a "Pollock"; etc. If you were Catholic, you were a "Crossback"; a Jew, a "Kike", and an Afro-American, a Negro. The majority of jokes targeted and strengthened these stereotypes. Much of this, I think, was residue of the media campaign during World War II to make a scapegoat of and malign people of German or Japanese descent. Feelings were very strong toward the right religion (the only path was yours). Inter-religious and inter-racial marriages were practically non-existent. Inter-ethnic marriages were frowned on, but tolerated if there was a common religion (or pregnancy).

Even within the student body there was a further stereotyping and pigeonholing. Those students that performed in the school plays or musicals were "fags" or "queers". If a boy was thought of as being homosexual (lesbians didn't exist then), he was a "queer". If you wore glasses, you were "four-eyes" and considered a nerd. If you didn't wear or embrace the current fad in clothing (boy or girl), you were a nerd. Dungarees (jeans), T-shirts, and black leather boots or jacket made you a "hood", and it was interesting how girls who "put out" and were easy to "feel up" were considered whores, loose, bad girls, an easy touch, and were maligned at every opportunity. I can't remember the studs that bragged about their conquests ever being anything but admired as male role models. It was a double standard. Girls were bad, but the guys were good guys.

Since it was so important to have some saving-accepting identity to survive in the cliques that existed in school, especially in my case, being poor and embarrassed by my home situation, I regretted the obstructions that occurred that prevented me from playing sports more. When I went out for freshman football, although making the team, I had to help my mother after school and on Saturdays with the laundromat she was managing. This need always made me feel guilty when I went out for the team, but I did. During my junior year of high school, I put my foot down and told my mother I was going out for football. Because I lacked self-confidence, instead of staying on the varsity team, I accepted the invitation of the J.V. coach, Mr. Brown, to play first string tackle for him. I was made captain of the team, and we went undefeated that season! However the last game of the season, I broke a bone in my right wrist. The school physician (who was also the president of the Mineola School Board) set it, but it never healed. Twice during my senior year I broke that wrist again playing football and lacrosse. So, between having to work and injuries, my involvement in athletics was minimized, but it helped me to be accepted as a lesser "jock".

A very fortunate "spin-off" came from my attempts to play sports. Mineola high school at that time had a practice in physical education (since all of the P.E. teachers were also coaches) that if you were playing on a team, you didn't have to participate in physical education classes. You were excused to study or help the teacher. The coaches got to know and supported the jocks. One of my coaches Bruce Gehrke, J.V. baseball, helped change the course of my life.

You will recall I was taking auto mechanics along with my friends. Well, one day I was working on a teacher's car putting on a new muffler (we often made cheap, minor repairs on teacher's cars as practical experience). I was on a dolly underneath the car. Mr. Gehrke happened to walk by the shop and pulled me out from under the car. I still remember the conversation.

"Cliff, what are you doing here?"

"I'm putting a new muffler on."

"I can see that. I mean you shouldn't be in auto shop. You should be taking a college prep program. Come with me right now to guidance, so we can change your program."

So, dirty overalls and grease, I went with Mr. Gehrke to the guidance office, where the paperwork was done to switch me to a college preparatory program when the semester ended. I'm still so grateful for this outreach and concern that I named my second son Bruce, for Mr. Gehrke. I only regret my high school guidance counselor didn't support and promote my interest in being a physician. But, I did all right academically and know how important a teacher is in the lives of his or her students. Mr. Gehrke's interest, and all the extra help in math from my teachers, convinced me to be a teacher, like them, who cares for kids and who rescues them.

Teachers have profound influence on their students, especially if they have poor adult role models at home and a dysfunctional family. Accepting and showing concern for the student as an individual means everything. To receive positive strokes, recognition, praise (albeit small), creates and maintains an inner emotional bank account that might never have been opened. It creates hope, and confidence. You learn that with hard work, you can transcend your circumstances. I was rescued by my teachers and wanted to become one, especially when I experienced some outstanding professors in college who increased my vision and created new worlds for me. I wonder if this reciprocity of caring is the primary reason many children aspire to become educators?

Dating was very important in high school. Couples that were going "steady" were considered special and seemed to have it made because of their commitment and loyalty to each other. Although I dated several wonderful girls during my sophomore, junior, and senior years, I found it hard to be in the mainstream as I didn't have a home I wanted to take my girlfriend to, had great difficulty getting my mother's car for a date, and seldom could afford a movie, dance, and the usual diner stop afterwards. Going to the junior and senior proms was a big deal, especially the senior prom, but the thought never crossed my mind. There was no way I could afford or think of asking for the money it would cost to attend, so I stayed home and made believe I didn't need to go. It's only a one-night fling that's soon forgotten. But for weeks after the events, I truly felt left out and hurt.

My favorite high school sweetheart was Jo, who was one grade behind me. Whenever I would get swept away by romantic music, like Jackie Gleason's mood music, Frank Sinatra, and Nat King Cole, I would always think of her. Unfortunately, when I went away to college, she fell in love with another Mineola High School guy who looked like Tab Hunter, a very handsome blonde young movie star. When I learned of this during my trip home at Thanksgiving, I was crushed. Fortunately, there were some wonderful girls I dated the rest of the year at Syracuse, especially Mary. However, I was neither ready nor ripe to pursue a serious relationship, so I could roll with it. Yet, I think the emotional power of our first experience with romantic love lives in us throughout our lives.

One of my best friends, Todd Beck, asked our immediate group friends, Ed, Ken, and me if we wanted to go with he and his father, a Hempstead High School teacher and coach, over Easter vacation (and later Thanksgiving) to visit relatives in Wellsville, New York. I saw it as a great escape and gladly said yes. Over the next three years, beginning with my sophomore year in high school, we made the long ride together to Wellsville. We stayed in Todd's Uncle Ray Gardner's house on Madison Street. The experience greatly affected me.

Todd's Uncle Ray and Aunt Mary were gracious and loving hosts. Ray had a great sense of humor and enjoyed having us around. I immediately "fell in love" with Todd's cousin Gretchen who I thought was the most beautiful girl I had ever seen. All during the years at Mineola High I pined for her and could never get really interested in any of the wonderful girls I dated (except for Jo).

Looking back, I think this fantasy love for Gretchen helped me rationalize a not too great "love life" compared to my friends. Perhaps that's why I identify with the fantasy loves in the lyric of the songs "Laura" and "Aubrey was her name." Wellsville brings back fond memories of woodchuck shooting in the spring, and deer hunting in the fall. Ray Gardner became my newest and dearest surrogate father, along with Mr. Beck.

I'll always be in "love" with Gretchen, Jo, "Laura," and "Aubrey". Fantasy and dreams serve a purpose. They preserve an ideal—real or imaginary. Something you can't have and perhaps shouldn't. In a manner of speaking, the strong emotional attachment remains, although it's only a dream of what might have been. They are a 3-D, HD wish, profound and very personal; a secret, fond sanctuary in your mind to escape to, temporarily; or an interesting paradox. You co-create a type of reality, if only for a wishful fantasy.

One of my most embarrassing moments occurred within the same hour during our second Easter visit to Wellsville. I had gone to the local Lutheran Church with Todd, Mr. Beck, and some of Mr. Gardner's family. We sat in the second pew from the front. Tradition and ritual at St. John's Lutheran Church in Williston Park was that the congregation stood at the beginning of the service and remained standing, singing along with the choir, while they walked to the front of the church. This practice was so much habit with me that when the choir started to walk toward the front, I, of course, stood up and was singing away for probably fifteen seconds, until

I realized no one else was standing but me! Different place, different procedures; embarrassing, but no big deal.

About thirty minutes later, right in the middle of the minister's sermon, I felt a foot pressing up against my right heel. I couldn't figure this out. Next, I feel a foot pressing up against my left heel. I didn't want to turn around to see what the problem was, or ask the person to get their feet off mine. But as time went on, the pressure on the back of both my feet was increasing to the point where, I could see the shoes and socks of the person behind me. It was time to turn around and see what was going on! What I saw was a young boy who was laying on the edge of his pew, unconscious. He had fainted during the sermon and slid under my pew. And here I had been kicking back at his feet to make him stop pushing mine! Fortunately, the church ushers had come to help this boy, and the minister stopped till he was removed. I thought the minister had stopped because he could see me kicking him under my pew. Was I glad to leave church that day!

Fortunately, I had three good friends I stayed close to during my high school years who were the bedrock (along with their parents) of my support system. Playing sports, despite the injuries, helped me to be accepted. I got another unexpected boost from my summer job between my junior and senior years. During the previous summer, I worked as a laborer for the Town of Old Hempstead Highway Department to help out at home. The town asked me if I would prefer working at Bar Beach in Roslyn. I assumed I'd be working as a laborer. So I said yes, preferring to be at a beach than being driven all over and sweltering on the blacktop streets in July and August.

When I arrived at Bar Beach, the weekend before Memorial Day, the chief lifeguard thought I was sent there by the town to be considered as a lifeguard. Another student Joe Smith, a senior at Chaminade High School and I were asked to go into the pavilion where we were given bathing suits to put on for our swimming test. Neither of us was prepared for this, but the opportunity was too good to pass up. Tom McKee, the chief lifeguard, walked with us out to the end of the pier that extended about fifty yards into Hempstead Harbor. He told us to swim out to a buoy (about 300 yards away), swim around it, and swim back. While the air was seventy degrees, the water had to be fifty-five degrees. I've never felt so cold in my life.

Despite not being a great swimmer, and spending a good deal of energy worrying about freezing to death or drowning, or the embarrassment of failure, I managed to stay behind Joe, and we both made it. We were informed we would be lifeguards beginning next weekend. I couldn't believe it...and was really excited about this new role! I'll never forget telling my friends I was going to be a lifeguard at popular Bar Beach for the summer (including weekends before school was over) and the jealous reactions I got, including questions about how they could apply. Suddenly, I had a popularity surge!

I worked as a lifeguard at Bar Beach for a total of six summers. The pay rate was $1.00 an hour. I was paid $1.10 an hour the year I was captain in 1958.

Tom McKee was a fascinating character, and an excellent trainer and chief lifeguard. Primarily what I remember about him are his numerous idiosyncrasies. Each morning he filled his gallon jug at the roadside spring in Roslyn; he kept the jug in the middle of the pavilion. He had lost his vision in one eye, so when he took a drink, he would always turn his body sideways and kept his good eye trained on the beach. Knowing that he never looked at the jug, one of the guards put two small, live goldfish in Tom's jug one morning. When he did notice the fish, still very much alive, at the end of the day, he laughed and said it was one of the best practical jokes ever played on him. We all thought he would go nuts on us.

Bar Beach was Tom's life. He would work in the off season in the maintenance shed near the entrance to the beach painting the lifeguard stands, wooden benches, etc., and getting everything ready for the next summer. He would always follow the same routines, day after day, month after month. When we arrived at the beach on Memorial Day, our first job was to place and anchor the two large wooden floats off the front of the pier that ran perpendicular to the beach. The floats had to go in exactly the same spot that they occupied in the map in Tom's mind. Some of us would be assigned to use the two lifeguard rowboats to maneuver the rafts to his exact anchoring spot. Tom would stay on each float, after carefully laying out the anchors, chain, and nuts and bolts, (which he greased during the winter.) One year, unfortunately "Hondo", one of our new lifeguards, inadvertently kicked one of the bolts over the side of the float. Tom went crazy.

"I've been using these same nuts and bolts for over twenty years and never had to request new ones. I'm not going to break my perfect record! Hondo, dive in and retrieve that bolt."

After fifteen minutes of unsuccessful dives, Hondo was beginning to suffer from hypothermia, so Tom let him quit. We all felt sorry for Hondo, but more so for Tom.

You could predict every move Tom McKee would make. He arrived at precisely the same time each morning, parked in the same spot, and ate lunch at the strike of noon, spreading out his lunch bucket in the same spot on the same bench. After eating, he would always ask if one of us wanted to play checkers. He always won.

The first instruction we got in the morning was "someone go into the first aid station and get the American flag." What other flag would there be? Tom's day off was Wednesday, which he would spend with his lady admirer who was the age of his mother. So, knowing his modus operandi, here's the plan we pulled off one Wednesday when we knew from the weather report the beach would be crowded. We developed an elaborate scheme to pull off a shark scare around 1:00 P.M., when the beach would be at capacity.

Just to the right of the pier, in front of the pavilion and refreshment stand, (usually the most crowded and popular spot on the beach), right in front of the lifeguard towers, we would:

1. Send one of the off duty lifeguards out from shore about fifty feet with a woman's white rubber bathing cap tucked in his suit to put on at the right time.

2. Another off-duty lifeguard would be in the water nearby with a concealed black swim flipper, which would be used to give the impression of a shark's dorsal fin while he swam underwater.

3. As the lifeguard on duty in the tower, I would point and draw the attention of the people around the stand to a "shark" attacking a "woman."

It was my idea to conceal a bottle of ketchup we obtained from the refreshment stand in the back of the rowboat (which had a flat surface for swimmers to be pulled on to), that we could put all over the "victim's" legs once we got him into the boat. Upon rowing back to shore, the captain on duty, as well as all other shore off-duty lifeguards, would gather around the rowboat to prevent people from getting a close look at the victim. Very loudly I would tell the captain that the woman I saw was not found. The captain of the lifeguards (usually a senior guard) would announce loudly to the crowd that he was calling an ambulance and the police to shut the beach. It didn't take much more than that. Within thirty minutes, maybe 100 people were left on the entire beach just sunbathing.

Although we feared this prank might reach the media, or Tom would find out about it, nothing happened. Good thing. Nobody noticed we were flying Cuba's flag that day, either. We had a ball and got away with it! The "shark fin" looked surprisingly real from a distance, and the bathing cap did the trick! And ketchup looks like blood, especially when diluted by salt water! It came off like a well-rehearsed movie scene! And, long before "Jaws!"

I was very fortunate to work with the lifeguards at Bar Beach. All were in college, many in the Ivy League, and they created a new support group and were encouraging and accepting of me. One of them, Brian Dennehy, went on to become a successful actor. All went on to successful professional careers. My new support group gave me the courage and challenging choices to overcome the restraining forces of my parents not wanting me to go to college and leave home. By accomplishing all the physically demanding life guard drills, achieving Red Cross Water Safety Instructor certification, my self concept and esteem were strengthened. I also obtained continuous summer work at local country clubs and camps during my seven years teaching. Further, I embedded the concept-goal of prevention in my habits, manifesting in being proactive throughout my personal life and professional career. These were the silver linings that accompany growth experiences that I couldn't see in their original context.

High school graduation was tough. Although I had been accepted to the New York State College of Forestry (SUNY) at Syracuse University and was looking forward to it, I'll never forget the strong emotions of loss and fear I experienced at and after the graduation ceremony. I looked around and realized all my friends, who had written such nice things in my yearbooks the last two years, would be gone. Even my friends that lived the closest to me would probably not be seen again.

Instead of being a happy experience, I was very estranged at the end of graduation day. Years later, at my college graduation ceremony, the feeling was relief. I received my degree, and since I was not as close to my college classmates as I had been to my high school friends, I felt little loss (probably because Hofstra was only a commuter campus then). High school graduation, in retrospect, was a more traumatic event in my life than graduating from college.

Twenty-five years later, I had an interesting serendipitous experience when I was interviewed by my former sixth-grade teacher, Ben Wallace, who was then the superintendent of the Mineola School System for the position of high school principal. I was glad I wasn't offered the position primarily because I liked living out on eastern Long Island and the relief that if any of my former high school teachers were still working, they couldn't believe I was going to be their boss. Whew—close call! But ego-boosting, though.

Attempt at Escape

Accepting Challenging Choices
Birth of a Dream
1954 – 1955

The real voyage of discovery consists not in seeking new landscapes, but in having new eyes.

- Marcel Proust

Far better it is to dare mighty things. To win glorious triumphs, even though checkered by failures, then to take rank with those poor spirits who neither enjoy much nor suffer much, because they live in the gray twilight that knows not victory or defeat.

- Theodore Roosevelt

———————————•———————————

Despite strong discouragement from my mother ("neither Gloria nor Phoebe went, and your father and I only went to the sixth grade"), in late August 1954, I left for Syracuse University with a high school friend who was a sophomore there and had a car. At that time, SUNY did not charge tuition (thank God). My upfront expenses for each semester was $60.00 in lab fees (returnable if no breakage), $88.00 for my dorm room, and $244 for the meal plan. Since I had expressed interest in playing lacrosse, the coach was able to get me a job washing dishes, which paid for my meals and dorm fees. My room was in Collendale, which was about seven miles away from campus—something I didn't know when I signed up for it. Thank God for my sister Gloria who sent me a check each week for $5.00 to cover laundry and incidental expenses!

Freshman orientation week was humiliating. You had to wear an orange beanie (I still have it) and put up with a lot of harassment from the upperclassmen. I still remember the convocation held for all freshman the Friday evening of orientation week. The president of the university and deans gave speeches and explained the motto of Syracuse: Suos Cultores Scienta Coronat [Knowledge Crowns those that Seek Her]. I was in awe at the challenge, and academic culture I experienced at that event.

A highlight of freshman orientation week for me was attending the special dance they had for us. I was lucky to get a date with a gorgeous blonde junior transfer student. As we entered the hall on campus, I was overwhelmed that the band playing live on stage was Les and Larry Elgart, my favorite band! Was I on a high that evening!

Although pumped up by the inspirational speeches I heard at the convocation, once I started my classes, I realized college was much different from high school! My schedule (nineteen credit hours) consisted of; inorganic chemistry and qualitative analysis, forest botany, college algebra and trigonometry, general forestry, engineering drawing, freshman English, public speaking, and army ROTC. I was soon overwhelmed with the demands of my schedule. Much time was spent in the chemistry and botany labs, as well as in ROTC drills.

It snowed almost every day from Thanksgiving until mid-April, which at times got depressing. During a fall intramural football game, I was clipped and landed on my coccyx bone, which is at the base of the spine. I thought I had broken it, and was taken to the infirmary where it was X-rayed. It was bruised, not fractured. Within two days, I came down with a 103-degree fever, and severe lower-back pain; I found myself back in the infirmary. The university athletic surgeon examined me and said the fall had caused an infection in a pilonidal cyst that I did not know I had at the base of my spine. With only local anesthetic, I remember the pain I felt when he lanced the cyst and then scraped out several hairs with the scalpel to "now prove his diagnosis." I spent the next three days in the infirmary taking sitz baths to drain the infection. Dr. Swift told me to have surgery over the Christmas break to remove the cyst, which I did. Much to my chagrin, it took <u>eight months</u> for the incision to heal! I was never able to play lacrosse in the spring, and between the pain I was in, trips to the infirmary for sitz baths, and bandaging the incision, washing dishes, and my studies, I was able to only pull a C average for my freshman year. Yet, a highlight for me was being elected president of my dormitory. I learned a great deal about people living in close quarters. It was a lesson in human relations and survival...but not an appropriate environment for studying. You are better off going to the library or any other quiet, private place.

When my mother and sister Phoebe came to pick me up in May, I was informed there had been a fire in the house, and the whole inside would have to be cleaned and painted. I would have to help at the house and could not go back to Syracuse. Further, my mother expected me to work full time and contribute fifty percent of my salary for living expenses. When my mother told me I had to discontinue my college ambitions, something inside told me this was wrong. I was still dependent and hadn't yet developed my inner strengths, so I went along with it for the next two years. During this time, I realized my two sisters didn't have lives. I vowed to myself that I would not succumb to her control and pressure, and would soon return to college full time and leave my dysfunctional family as soon as I could.

While heartbroken, I accepted my fate and went over to nearby Hofstra College in Hempstead, where I was accepted as a part-time student for the next two years and ultimately, by getting good grades, was given an academic scholarship based on financial need. I found Hofstra to be on an academic par with Syracuse, and even then my new challenging choice was to finish college, no matter how many obstacles were put in my way.

As I now look back on my freshmen year, I value being an "Orangeman" even though only for two semesters, and the memory of having Jim Brown in my ROTC platoon. (I knew Jim from speaking with him at Bar Beach and playing against him in lacrosse.) But I don't miss the winter there. You get tired of the cold and snow. The weather can change several times within an hour.

The college of forestry was a four-year undergraduate program when I attended. It changed its program and name in the 1980s to the NY State State College of Environmental Sciences and Forestry, admitting students into their junior year. It is one of the best in the country. While I wished I could have continued there, things worked out in the long run, as you'll see.

New Directions

Accepting Change
Staying on Course
1955 – 1957

Courage is not simply one of the virtues, but the form of every virtue at the testing point.

- C.S. Lewis

The richness of the human experience would lose something of rewarding joy if there were no limitations to overcome.

- Helen Keller

———————————●———————————

For the next two years, 1955-57, I worked full time for the town of Old Hempstead Highway Department as a sign painter, from September to May and in the summers, I was back at Bar Beach as a lifeguard, working the late shift so I could take two courses at Hofstra College in the morning. During the two years, I was able to take thirty-six credits and, when I returned full time at Hofstra in September 1957, I was a junior—so I only "lost" one year.

Working for the highway department was an eye-opening learning experience. The first crew I was assigned to painted streets marking (SLOW, CAUTION, etc.), as well as striping the medians. The foreman was "Duke", and after a year, I realized he was illiterate. I never learned his real name. He insisted on being called the "Duke". Then there was "Monkey Face" Sam, so named because he always wore a fresh band-aid over the tip of his nose, which, according to him, had been bitten off in a childhood fight. Next was "Leadpipe" Lindsey and "Doc" Marino, who was a college graduate, with two years of medical school behind him before an alleged personal problem forced him to drop out, and me.

Whenever Duke was angry with us (which was often), he would call us "apes." Because he knew "Doc" was college educated, and I was going to college, we were called "educated apes." I loved that. After working with Duke's crew for three months, I was reassigned to work with Chick to paint and repair street signs, which were constantly in need of work.

I still don't know how Chick managed to do his job, as I soon found out he was illiterate. We had a pickup truck and pretty much followed our own work schedule. I loved the job, although our work station was a loft in the truck garage with no heat, except a small electric heater to get the small work area to just about fifty degrees, so we could paint and letter the signs. It suited me fine though, as I could even manage to study during lunch and breaks.

One spring morning Chick sent me to Westbury to put up some street signs. As I was driving through Carle Place, I came across Duke and the boys, who had just finished painting safety markings on the street in front of an elementary school. I immediately noticed the six-foot letters spelled out SLOW, and then ten feet farther away, SCOOL. I couldn't let this go by…I could just see the picture in Newsday and hear the fallout from the highway superintendent. So I pulled over to the side of the road and showed Doc. At first, much to my surprise, he didn't see the missing H. As soon as he did, he asked for my advice on how to tell the Duke, since he wouldn't know it was spelled wrong and would go ballistic when he realized it was a problem.

Realizing Doc was right, and since I knew I would catch hell for pointing out the mistake, and really didn't want to be called an "educated ape" again, I suggested that Doc take a can of paint thinner and accidentally spill it on the S and C, and use street sweeping brooms to make room for the H. He thought that was a good idea and decided not to tell Duke about the situation, since he wouldn't see a problem anyway. The next day, Doc saw me at the garage and told me Duke was sleeping through the incident and the correction was done by the boys. He thanked me and couldn't believe he didn't see the spelling error. I was just glad it didn't make it to Channel 12 or Newsday! But then again, perhaps no one would have noticed.

Whenever there was a weather report of a serious snowstorm, all the workers at the highway department garage had to stay to man the trucks with plows and/or shovel snow. Most of us didn't mind not going home because overtime pay was seldom and welcome. During this one terrible blizzard that started in the afternoon, I was assigned to stay and go out with Joe to work the hydraulic plow on his huge ten-wheeler. What an experience!

We left the garage about 6:30 P.M. and proceeded to Roslyn Road to plow it and the surrounding streets. I don't ever remember a snowstorm as bad on Long Island. The snow was well over a foot deep and heading for two. The drifts made it appear much worse. The winds made the situation treacherous. What was bothering me more than the cold was my safety and concern for Joe. He would stop in every bar we passed to ask if they wanted their parking lot plowed. Most said yes, and in addition to getting a few bucks (I never saw any of it), he would accept a free boilermaker. After doing a lot of bar and grill parking lots, I do not know how Joe could drive, since he had consumed God knows how many boilermakers.

Although I was worried about Joe's condition, and possibly being reported for plowing out private property, (there were large Town of Old Hempstead Highway Department decals on both truck doors), his driving ability did not change. I just sensed he was mellow. Around 1:30 A.M., with the blizzard conditions getting worse, and at least two feet of snow drifts now on the ground, we started to plow the streets in the industrial park off Roslyn Road. As we were going down a hill, I noticed what appeared to be a car buried in snow ahead of us. It was hard to tell because the snow was so deep. I told Joe to stop because I wanted to get out and check the car since it shouldn't be parked in this nonresidential area, far from the main roads. Reluctantly,

Joe stopped. I got out and plowed my way to the driver's side of the car. I pushed away the snow, and much to my surprise, the window rolled down. I could see a young black man and woman next to him and another black couple in the backseat. They were stranded and consequently thrilled and excited that we found them. I told them we were plowing the streets for the Town of Old Hempstead Highway Department, and we would help them.

So I went back to the truck and told Joe what I had found in the car. He told me to find out how much money they had to pay for his services. I thought to myself that he was kidding—how can a public servant, especially in time of need, ask for money for what should be a free service. But I knew better and went back to the car, and using my best diplomacy explained my (our) problem with the truck driver, hoping they would understand. They pooled their money, which was all loose change, and offered me $1.37. I couldn't take it. So, I went back to the truck and explained to Joe that all they had was a $1.37 in change.

"Cliffee," he called to me. "Go back to the car and tell them that if all they have is a dollar thirty-seven, then we want their women! I could use my luck being changed."

I couldn't believe this noble humanitarian. Change his luck? I hadn't even had any luck yet, and I wasn't about to go back to the car and ask for their women! So I drew the line and told Joe he was nuts. They were stranded in this blizzard, and it was our duty to help them. It was bad enough we expected a "tip" to help them, but to ask for the services of their women was too much! What would we do, switch spots and go into a freezing car? Plus, I was worried about agitating the two men and not knowing what they might do. I also told Joe that we could lose our jobs if we were reported for how we treated them. He finally agreed but wanted the money. So I went back to the car, and somehow mustered the courage to ask for it. Fortunately, they were so grateful to be "rescued" that they all apologized they didn't have any more.

I went back to the truck and gave Joe the $1.37 in change. He told me to get the chain out that was under my seat. I remember never seeing such large chain links and huge hooks on either end. It was so heavy that I could just about move the chain out of the truck. The car was just part of a drift. I had no sure way of knowing where I was placing the hook. Reaching through the snow, I secured the hook under the rear bumper, figuring that would pull the car out. I walked over to the truck and hooked the other end on the coupling on the front bottom of the truck. I signaled Joe to back up, which he did. I soon had to shout, "stop," as the car barely moved, but the entire rear bumper came off the car!

I figured that I'd better find a more secure part of the chassis, but I still couldn't be sure, with all the snow around, over, and under the car. Finally, after feeling for something solid, I placed the hook on metal and told Joe to back up. Again, I soon shouted to "stop," as this time, with little movement of the car, we had managed to pull off the left rear fender! The chain was not going to work!

Hoping the male occupants would not get out of the car to survey the damage, I made my way back to the truck to determine a different rescue technique. Joe said the only other way to move the car was to use the plow because the snow was too deep. I got back into the truck. So he backed up about fifty feet, told me to drop the plow, and we rammed the rear, going about ten miles per hour. The huge headlights on the top of the trucks cab, as well as front fenders, showed the snow cascade off the top. Now we could see that we had pushed in the rear end. You could see the trunk collapsed. Joe pushed the car almost to the end of the dead-end street. I couldn't imagine what he was thinking. I soon found out.

He stopped and backed up. We plowed our way past the car, managed to turn around, so now we were facing the front of the car. Joe backed up again, accelerated to about ten miles per hour, told me to drop the plow, and we rammed the front of the car, collapsing the front fenders and grill into the motor! But the car was moving, and we were pushing it to the top incline where the first crossroad was. When we got to the top, Joe stopped and backed up. He pulled away to the right telling me we were going to plow these streets. I couldn't believe he was going to leave these people stranded, with a ruined car that probably wouldn't start because the front was pushed in so the motor probably wouldn't start. So I told Joe we couldn't leave them, as they could still be stranded. He replied, "What the fuck do they want for a $1.37!"

Nice guy! I'll never forget his comment and can't believe the couples didn't report us for damage to their car or leaving them in the middle of a blizzard! I was afraid I'd lose my job. Around 5:00 A.M. we pulled into the highway department yard, our plowing done. Joe was drunk (he finished the six pack he got from the last bar we plowed). I was exhausted, embarrassed, and worried. But the incident was never reported—at least not to my knowledge. But I'll, certainly never forget my failed rescue attempts, another lesson in physics, and the importance of sound character.

Renewal – Rebirth

Achieving Goals
Completing College
1957 – 1959

The ultimate measure of a man is not where he stands in moments of comfort and convenience, but where he stands at times of challenge and controversy.

- Martin Luther King Jr.

Yesterday is history, tomorrow is a mystery, and today is a gift; that's why they call it the present.

- Eleanor Roosevelt

In September of 1957, I was able to return to Hofstra College full time, thanks to a scholarship based on financial need and my B average. Hofstra would grow and become the outstanding university it is today. The campus is now more than twice the size and no longer a "commuter college." I'm very proud to be a Hofstra alumnus—and very grateful!

One beautiful coed in my educational psychology class caught my eye. Her name was Geri, and we dated the next three semesters. I was attracted by her looks, the way she dressed, and her reserved demeanor. She smiled and laughed easily. I liked that. I became infatuated with her. She had class. She accepted me. She seemed to have similar goals and outlooks on life. We found that we had the same blood type and were born on the twenty-first (me in May and Geri in December). This seemed to imply we were meant to be. Typical adolescent romantic love. Coupled with being in the artificial world of college (highly structured, safe, secure, isolated, and protected from reality) every-thing looks rosy and ideal. We should have met later, when we had at least one foot in the adult, real world. Perhaps we both wanted to leave our homes and grabbed at the first opportunity for escape. I know I did.

We were married in June 1959. Looking back on our 19 year marriage, now, over those years, I felt we no longer liked each other as when we were dating. We had four wonder-ful children, though, Brian, Cynthia, Bruce, and Susan. She was a good mother. Her parents were great in-laws. They supported us. Henry, her father, became another surrogate dad for me. More about the marriage later.

Since I already had a strong foundation in the sci-ences (from my first year at Syracuse's College of Forestry), I decided to major in English and minor in biology. My tran-script would show thirty-six hours in both science and English courses, so I would be certified in both subjects. I knew I wanted to teach, but wasn't sure if it was English, or science. I had an outstanding English professor at Syracuse and found the English professors at Hofstra equally stimulating (almost like philosophy courses). Between the excellent professors I had at Syracuse and Hofstra, I knew teaching was going to be my career. In my senior year, I decided I didn't want to teach English, especially grammar, and that my real interest was biology or general science.

My main ambition was to teach, and to be with kids and other educated adults. I knew what it had done for me and wanted to continue enjoying both the content and process of teaching. There's nothing like the gratification of teach-ing—the interaction, being creative, thinking on your feet, and being your own boss in your classroom. You enjoy the autonomy and spontaneity.

I did my student teaching in biology at the Wheatley School, a public high school in the East Williston School dis-trict. The students were from lower-upper-class and upper-middle-class communities and approximately 90 percent went on to college. It was a wonderful school, almost like a private preparatory, but not a realistic experience to prepare me for Isle of Trees Junior High School, where the students came from the middle-class communities of Levittown, Bethpage, Seaford, and Plainedge.

In early 1959, when I realized I was going to get married and reflected on the impact the different religions (Geri was Catholic, and I, Lutheran) would have on our children, especially these two opposing doctrines. I still remember, as a kid, hearing Catholics called "Crossbacks" and Catholics swearing all other religions (even though Christian) were doomed to hell. Because I knew Martin Luther had been a Catholic priest, and the Lutheran Church service was very similar to the Catholic mass, I decided to convert to Catholicism. When I told my mother I was going to do this, she carried on for months that I was a traitor, and now I would be going to hell! She cried everyday (in front of me, anyway) and would claim I was causing her to get migraine headaches. I survived her sabotage, however, and completed my instructions to convert. Another challenging choice to transcend my mother's need to control.

Father Murphy was an excellent teacher. His conversion class was composed of two students, a Protestant bride to be and me. He would remind us that the final choice to become Catholic was ours and not to feel bad if, at the end, we decided not to convert. At the end of my last session, the bride decided not to go further, but I told Father Murphy I wanted to become a Catholic, as I saw many more similarities to Lutheranism than differences. He was pleased with both of us and told me to meet with him next week to get prepared for confession and to become confirmed. Little did I know what I was getting into!

After the session on how to do confession, I thought I was prepared. However, now that I was sitting in the church pew about to go into the confessional next, my heart was pumping out of my chest and I was beyond anxious. It was now my turn! As I went into the confessional booth, I noticed a microphone hanging on the wall by the screened window where you kneel by the priest. As I pulled back the thick velvet curtain, I said to my self, "Why didn't Father Murphy mention the microphone to me? Probably because it wasn't needed to point it out, or he forgot." So I took the "microphone" off the hook and held it in front of my lips. The priest rolls back the window partition, and I see him sitting, waiting for me to start. So I say, "Bless me, father. This is my first confession."

"I can't hear you, speak louder."

"Bless me, father. This is my first confession." He now replies louder (interrupting me)...

"I don't know what you're speaking into, but your voice is very garbled and I can't hear you. Speak up. Louder."

No, that didn't sound like a good idea. So I told him, "Father, I don't think it will help if I speak louder. I think you need to turn on the speaker in there so you can hear me. I'm speaking into the microphone."

His reply was the most embarrassing moment in my life, "My son, there is no speaker in here. You are talking into the hearing aid for people who are hard of hearing."

I wanted to leave, but was frozen with embarrassment and anxiety. Fortunately, the rest of the confession went better, and I survived my first experience.

I had been a Catholic for about two months and decided to stop at confession in Syosset with Ron Como (Perry's son) on our way home from work one Saturday night. I felt more relaxed in that I wouldn't make an ass out of myself this time, as I now knew about the hearing aid and would leave it there. I was about, however, to have a much worse experience.

After the priest opened the confessional window, I said in a normal volume, "Father, bless me. This is my second confession."

"Tell me your sins, my child."

So far so good. I started out with "I missed mass last Sunday." Before I could go on with my short list, he said, (Interrupting me)...

"Did you say you missed mass?", getting louder with each word.

"Yes, I work at the Country Club as a lifeguard and had to be at work at eight o'clock that morning."

"Well, let me tell you something, son!" he said, his loud voice getting louder and angrier. "You could have gone to the six o'clock or the seven o'clock morning mass or evening mass on Saturday!" Now he bellowed at me, "Do you know your soul is now roasting in hell because you missed mass?"

I knew every parishioner in the pews could hear him and was wondering if I had murdered the pope. I couldn't handle his comment. So I told him since I was still alive, I couldn't believe my soul was in hell, and got up, left the church, and didn't go back to confession ever again. Coming from a Lutheran background, I didn't need a priest phone booth to communicate with God. I also wanted a more forgiving, loving listener. I remained a Catholic on the surface for my marriage and children. I wanted us all to be headed in the same direction on Sundays. However, the longer I was bored with the same routine rituals of the mass and especially poor homilies, I was being turned off by what I felt were meaningless experiences.

Churches are man made, but spirituality is God given. Years later, I still went to mass but only out of social necessity. I'm now looking for a Christian church where I can feel at peace and spiritual. No more stand up, sit down, kneel, and watch the priest do all the thinking for everybody. I still find it interesting when in certain situations, like being admitted to a hospital, you're asked, "What religion are you?" I reply, "Christian." But then I'm asked "What kind?" Why can't Christian suffice...do I have to be the right brand? I still feel more spiritual when I'm outdoors sensing magnificent nature, then I do in a very structured church service that emphasizes the negative, dark shadow of human nature and God.

New Beginnings

Start of Marriage and Teaching
1959–1966

Lord, grant that I may always desire more than I accomplish.

- Michelangelo

We must be the change we wish to see in the world.

- Gandhi

Courage is fear that has said its prayers.

-Dorothy Bernard

Upon graduation in May 1959, I began my education career in the Isle of Trees Junior High School, teaching general science in grades seven through nine. The school district had no church, library, or post office. It was a "bedroom community" and very political at the time. My teaching salary was $4,500. I received $200 for coaching freshmen football. The money was meager, but the experiences great. Here are a few.

Before Labor Day weekend, I attended a two-day orientation for new teachers, where we were given survival-success advice by the principal, assistant principal, and several veteran teachers. We were cautioned to be the boss, to seize immediate control, and to be tough as nails. One vet, (my science department chairperson) implored us to "not smile until Christmas." While I thought the comment a bit excessive, the warning was helpful in creating a mindset not to be a friend too soon, or middle school kids would misinterpret your need for authority. Training was as important as teaching subject matter. They were right. Students need to be *trained* to the culture—they need classroom habits (learned behavior) before you can teach effectively. Primary student behaviors that are essential for the teaching-learning process are; to pay attention, respect each other, and ask questions if you don't understand something.

I emphasized teaching critical-creative thinking skills and encouraged asking questions. Learning to ask higher-level, insightful questions that challenge a concept's validity is an important tool in scientific progress and in understanding life's mysteries. It made teaching science more interesting for me, and I hope, for my students.

After the first two weeks of football practice, we had our first scrimmage with another school. I would send in players to assume certain positions, but they would go out onto the field and look around, not knowing a tackle from a linebacker or safety location. So at the end of practice, I called all of the seventh and eighth grade boys together and gave them a real Knute Rockne lecture about knowing where every position is, since I didn't know yet for sure, who was going to play what, or on offense or defense. So I told them all to go home and think about football...nothing but football, and come back the next day knowing where each position is, so they could find their correct spot on the field. I thought I did a great job!

However, that next afternoon, as we were getting ready for practice, there was a knock at the door of the coaches' room. One of the coaches answered the door and told me one of my players wanted to come in and talk with me. I said, "Okay." In came Walter, one of my seventh grade boys. Picture this conversation going on in front of all the coaches (freshman, J.V., and Varsity).

"Yes, Walter, what's up?"

"Mr. Bennett, you remember how yesterday after practice you told us all to go home and think about football?"

"Yes, Walter, I do. What about it?" I asked.

He held his hands up in front of his chest, creating the size and shape of a football, and said "Mr. Bennett, it's about this big."

I don't remember if the other coaches laughed out loud. I know I didn't want to embarrass Walter, so I said, "Good job, Walter. Now go get into your pads, and I'll see you outside." You can probably guess the kind of season we had (0-6), especially since the J.V. stole all my good players (my ninth graders) before the season started.

I coached one more year and went four -two that season. Despite the winning record, I found the job requirements too much. After our games on Saturday mornings, I was expected to scout for the varsity coach. I went to see the team he would play two weeks in advance. I would take notes and give recommendations on what defense to use and what plays might work on offense. I never got to see our varsity play. I figured out the total number of hours I was putting in at practice, driving students to the school physician after games, scouting on Saturday afternoons, and my pay came to about twenty-two cents an hour. I realized that while I <u>loved</u> coaching, I had to get a better paying part-time job. When I finished my master's degree at Hofstra in 1961, I was offered a job as an adjunct faculty member and began teaching education courses in the evening and on Saturday morning. The pay was much better, the work far more rewarding, and it benefited my résumé.

One place I avoided as much as possible at work was the faculty room. Teachers used it primarily to complain and bitch. I called it the "Ain't It Awful Room" because the conversations were about how awful a student, parent, or administrator was. After a while, you just don't want to go into an environment that's so negative and pessimistic; although I suppose much of the chatter is necessary catharsis. You want to go someplace where your thoughts will be reformed, not reinforced. You want to smile, to laugh, and to rejuvenate.

I usually went into the phys. ed. office before students arrived each morning for a cup of coffee because the group that met there were fun and upbeat. The small talk one morning was about an incident that happened at the high school the day before in twelfth grade English honors class. Apparently the focus of the course was creative writing. The teacher would usually give the students some kind of trigger (picture, sentence, image, poem, etc.), to motivate and stimulate the creative process. He was resting during his prep period in the English Department office when all of a sudden he realized there was just ten minutes before the start of his class. So he grabbed a ditto master and hurriedly typed; the pen is mightier than the sword...or so he thought. He quickly ran off twenty copies, and just made it to class on time.

After distributing the trigger of the day to the class, he couldn't understand the laughter and giggles coming from the students. Knowing it was coming from the ditto he had just given out, he quickly looked at it. He hadn't hit the space bar between *pen* and *is*. Need I say more? Good thing they were seniors and good kids. Other than some embarrassment, (and ribbing from his colleagues) apparently nothing more came from his haste. Hell of a trigger, though!

Some more anecdotes from my teaching years at Isle of Trees. I developed an interesting lab activity for teaching Archimedes principle (also known as specific density.) I used the displacement of water method (same way Archimedes discovered the idea) and weighing in air. The students were required to plot out the results on graph paper, which showed the different masses of the same specimens had the same specific density, as seen by the straight line on the graph. I was very proud of my technique and thought I had done a great job teaching the concept. Until I read one test paper. I used definitions a lot; I hate short answer tests because knowing a word does not mean understanding. One paper had the following definition for the Archimedes principle: "The man in charge of the school Archimedes went to." I couldn't believe it. So I looked in my grade book and was glad to see the student had been absent that lesson. I gave him partial credit for a clever answer.

General Science, when I first started at Isle of Trees, was taught for only one half a year in grades seven and eight. One of my students that I had the first half of the year responded to my request to loan interesting science related objects for our classroom by bringing in his tonsils in a glass jar, which I put in my back glass-covered storage cabinet. Needless to say, I forgot about his tonsils. He didn't.

On the last day of school in June, in the late morning on the bus platform (I had bus duty), he walked up to me and said, "Mr. Bennett, could I please have my tonsils? I want to take them home with me." He held his hand out. I had to tell him I didn't carry them around with me, and he would have to get them from me at another time since they were still in the classroom. He got them the first day of school in September. Be prepared.

One of my monthly routine lessons was to have the students bring in a report from a current newspaper or magazine that explained a new scientific or technical discovery. I wanted them to see the significance of science and technology in practical ways in everyday life. I'll never forget one seventh grade boy getting up in the front of the classroom and reading out loud his article from a newspaper. He read, "Science makes new discovery to help h-e-m-o-r-r-h-o-i-d-s." He had to spell the unfamiliar word. I immediately realized this was a lead in for an advertisement for a treatment and told the student to bring me the article. I knew the students either couldn't understand him or realized what he spelled. I gently thanked him for the article but explained this wasn't the type of news we wanted, it was an advertisement that used the word science in it. I don't think he understood, but the incident caused me to subscribe to a monthly age-appropriate magazine we reviewed together in class. I guess it could have been worse—especially today.

My best "gotcha" came to me spontaneously during one of my seventh grade science classes. Before the lesson started, one of my boys gave me an apple. My antenna immediately went up because male middle school students no longer bring teachers gifts, not even an apple. I noticed the skin had been cut around the stem, and there was a slight yellow brownish color around this edge. After thanking him, I thought, "I'll get ya!" So I immediately postponed the start of the lesson, took out a beaker, and filled it with water. I lit the Bunsen burner and put a beaker holder over the flame. The students were all wondering if this was going to be my demonstration for today's lesson. I announced that one of them had given me an apple, and I was going to put it through a "scientific analysis." I cut the apple into pieces, and as I expected, mustard (I hoped) had been put into the space where the core was. I explained I was going to put in a chemical compound (potassium permanganate) to test if this substance in the apple had combined to make poison. I knew the liquid would turn purple and remain so. But I told the class that if the color turns to a bright red after two hours (dismissal time), then the purple color was changed by whatever was put in the apple. This meant "poison" was present, and it was a good thing I didn't eat it.

I left the Bunsen burner on low and went on with my lesson. Most students paid attention to me, but some, especially the gift bearer, remained mesmerized by the slowly boiling purple water and apple. It worked like a charm! I knew at dismissal time, who would come back to my room to see if he might have been a murderer. He came into my room, looked at the purple beaker, and breathed a big sigh of relief. He apologized to me for putting the mustard in the apple. I accepted his apology but told him to think through pranks about possible consequences. We both felt relieved. He for not committing a "crime" and me for knowing that yellow-brown color was only mustard ... and for seizing the teachable moment!

Another student thought my knowledge of science extended to veterinary medicine. He came back to school one afternoon with his wounded pigeon.

"Please fix him, Mr. Bennett."

I tried to explain that I wasn't a vet, but I also didn't want him to think I wasn't concerned, so I took the bird, which he told me couldn't fly because his wing was broken. I looked inside the folded wing and, seeing the wound looked healed, I carefully pulled the scab off that was stuck on the feathers. I told the student maybe he would be all right, take him home, and if he couldn't fly, to take him to a vet. He came back the next morning, all smiles, and told me the bird was flying. He thought I was a miracle worker. If only everything was that easy!

Our society promotes immediate gratification of the senses. Children and especially teenagers live in a world of continuous multisensory stimuli. This conditioning heightens boredom if the senses are all not engaged, constantly. Imagine what it takes for a teacher to keep students on task that is not always fun, electronic, and "interesting." It gets harder each year to keep students attention.

Being an effective teacher requires a combination of knowledge, skills, and talents. First and foremost is knowing your content (subject matter) and being truly interested in it, indeed, passionate, about it. Then comes the creativity to make your lesson experience enjoyable for the students. Throughout the lesson you need to vary your methodologies (teaching-learning activities) so you touch all the students learning modalities. Humor helps, as does a world of patience. Throw in concern for classroom dynamics (order, control, and discipline) and time management for nitty-gritty reality. An endless supply of energy is required for this work. But the look in the faces of the students when they enjoy your class is worth it. Teachers should get more praise, pay, and appreciation from the public. You have no idea how draining and all consuming the demands are from inside and outside (parents) the classroom.

During a class, a student suddenly opened the door and exclaimed, "Mr. Bennett, there is a fire in the wall outside here in the hall!" Of course, I leave immediately and find smoke coming from a garbage-trash receptacle (which were recessed in the walls) by each staircase, top and bottom. So I grabbed the nearest fire extinguisher, burning my hand as I pushed in the metal flap to insert the hose. I felt I had quenched the fire and returned to my room, immediately calling the main office to alert our head custodian to be sure the fire was out. Within ten minutes, while still teaching the same class, another student opens the door and reports the same situation except this time, it's at the bottom of the stair well about twenty feet away. So I repeat my performance. As I'm spraying the trash receptacle with a soda acid water extinguisher (again burning my hand), the Principal Ernie V. comes down the stairs with a new teacher candidate he was taking on a tour of the school. Embarrassed, he says to me, "What are you doing Mr. Bennett?

I replied, "I'm putting out a fire, Mr. V."

He turns to the prospective young teacher and says, "This doesn't happen very often here." Great answer! My hand healed, and I was reimbursed for my clothes, which sprouted holes from the acid-water mix. I never saw the prospective teacher again. If he was offered a position, his hallway experience probably scared him away. And I was never thanked for putting out the potential fires.

Where there is a will, there is a way. The ninth grade class pressed the principal to allow a picnic at Belmont Lake State Park, and he approved it. This was held on the last day of classes before final exams. Everything seemed fine, there was no outlandish dress, and the climate seemed okay for this outing. Several other teachers and I noticed that many students were bringing whole watermelons. We became really suspicious when we observed very little picnic food being eaten. However, the kids were putting away the watermelon.

By noon, there was none left. It was around this time we were also noticing several students acting a little tipsy. We had searched their picnic baskets and any carrying cases they had before getting on the buses, hoping to confiscate beer or booze before we got to the park. We had found nothing. The kids, as usual, were one step ahead of us. They had injected the watermelons with vodka before leaving home! Fortunately, no one fell in the lake and there was no one really drunk (thank God). The behavior was not punished, but noted for future searches or concealments. Oh, the joys of chaperoning!

Learning to develop an effective practice of classroom control-management was essential. Fortunately for me, I didn't realize how much help I received from just being the freshman football coach. This role added a dimension of respect and recognition that a first year teacher usually doesn't have. My style, when students weren't paying attention or talking, was to stop speaking and wait for feedback from the students (verbal and nonverbal) to make them realize the focus was now on them. They would turn or stop, look at me and realize from my body language I was miffed. I would always send an "US" message so the students realized we had to work as a team "Thanks, John, we need your help, too. We appreciate your understanding." I never had to raise my voice or send a student to the office for "discipline," which cannot come from without. The we plural pronoun worked like magic. It prevented me-them escalation and brought us closer. Lowering your voice also got their attention, I never shouted. During my seven years as a teacher, I never sent a student to the office to solve a problem between us. I'm proud of that.

Another technique I used often, which most students didn't even know I was doing, was to adjust the flame of the Bunsen burner so the colors would change. It would bring them back from daydream land. The Bunsen burner became a teaching tool for me. Worked like a charm.

During my second year at Isle of Trees, a fortunate series of events occurred that ended up benefiting me. Both were serendipitous. The science department chairperson, resigned to raise her family. The superintendent of schools had replaced her with a colleague-friend from upstate. The arrangement (unknown to us) was that he had resigned from being superintendent of schools upstate and had come down to be near Levittown where he was to assume the superintendency in January. This left an opening for the chairperson, which the principal asked me to take. Of course, I did—it paid an extra $500.00 a year, and you only taught three classes! This greatly helped, as I never had enough time to study for the graduate work I was doing at the time.

During a cold January in 1963, my father died at home. I was saddened by his passing; perhaps more so over not losing my father, but never knowing a dad. He had beaten cancer. He succumbed to heart failure.

We had three children while I taught at Isle of Trees, Brian was born March, 1960, in September, 1963 my daughter Cynthia was born, and Bruce in May, 1965.

Here's a cute anecdote that involved my son Brian when he was four years old. He had outgrown his only pair of pajamas. So, being frugal parents, when we purchased new ones, we purposely picked longer ones so he could grow into them and get more mileage. The ones he had been wearing were about four inches short at the wrists and ankles. He was used to that look and length. So when we put on the new ones, the sleeves were now down to his knuckles and the pant legs almost touched his toes. As soon as he looked himself over, he started crying hysterically.

We tried to console him asking what was hurting (they certainly weren't too small to pinch)? He couldn't talk, just kept crying. So we took off the pajamas, to see if maybe a straight pin was caught in the fabric and sticking him. There were no pins or anything else we could find that might cause discomfort. So, we put them back on. Now, he was crying louder than before. Since he was so upset, I got down on the floor and hugged him, reassuring there was nothing wrong with the PJs.

Finally, after several minutes of hugging, drying his tears, and trying my best to calm him down, he finally explained what his problem was: " I shrunk!" he exclaimed.

So we rolled up the sleeves and pant bottoms so he could see his former self. This worked. He relaxed and accepted his transformation. A very interesting perception and paradigm shift had occurred for us all.

In 1966, I finished my professional diploma in educational administration at Queens College, and left Isle of Trees at the end of the '65-'66 school year to become an assistant principal at a Suffolk County High School. The graduate school at Queens College (City University of New York) was outstanding. All the professors expected academic excellence and were experienced teachers and administrators. Their preparation was a great help for what was to come. I had achieved one of my challenging choices—getting into school administration!

Moving on Up?

Adjusting to School Administration
High School Assistant Principal
1966 – 1967

The quality of a man's life is in direct proportion to his commitment to excellence, regardless of his chosen field of endeavor.

- Vince Lombardi

The future belongs to those who believe in the beauty of their dreams.

- Eleanor Roosevelt

———————————— • ————————————

When I arrived as the new high school assistant principal in a South Shore Suffolk County School district, August 1, 1966, I received a cold reception from the principal, Frank J. I soon found out via feedback from colleagues that he had wanted one of his physical education teachers to be his new assistant, but was told by the superintendent that he had to take me, an outsider. Not a great start, but Frank soon became friendlier as soon as the school year started. Actually, as it turned out, I learned a lot from him about being an administrator, making tough decisions, and learning to say NO when needed. He had some interesting vernacular expressions when he got upset, calling someone a "lunch wagon" or "hairbag." He loved the F-word and used it often. When he was hot, you had to calm him down, especially if he was about to get on the P.A. to call a student to the office. He was fun to work for because he was very human, open, and emotional. He became a surrogate father and friend.

On the first day of school, I was patrolling the parking lot to ensure students were driving safely and parking in proper places. Right after the late bell rang, in pulls a car and the driver rides right into a huge pile of sand that was there for the winter snow. I went over and asked the young man to please move his car and park it in one of the other many available spaces. He mumbled something under his breath, backed up rapidly, hit the gas, and I got sprayed with sand. So I took him to my office, asked his name, and for his fathers work number so I could call and inform him of his son's behavior. I was going to suspend him for one day. (I checked with Frank first for permission, since technically only the principal can suspend a student, and he approved.) I called the number he gave me, which was one of the middle schools in the district. What I didn't realize was that his father was the principal! Although embarrassed because I didn't yet know the name, I didn't back down on my decision, and his father said send him home and apologized for his behavior. Not a great way to start a new job as an administrator, but the word got around quickly not to screw up with that new, young Assistant Principal Bennett...he even suspended a fellow principal's son!

One of my duties was being sure we held the required number of fire drills (twelve a year—eight before Christmas and the rest during the spring). The fire alarm was hooked up directly to the Fire Department, so you had to call first to let them know what time you were having the drill. Unfortunately, on the fifth drill of the fall, even though I always checked with Frank for approval for the time of the drill, I forgot to call the fire department. Needless to say, the trucks came in full force, and the students thought it was the real thing. Although very embarrassed at my error, it was probably the best drill of the year, and I never forgot to call again!

After suspending a boy for smoking in school, I received a phone call from the vice president of the school board who had just gotten a call from the boy's father who claimed I was prejudiced against Italians (I had also suspended the brother earlier in the year). I assured the board member I was not prejudiced, that the suspension is a requirement, as printed in the student handbook, and I reminded him, was also a policy of the Board of Education. He backed off and went along with my decision, but it was my first of many lessons in local political pressure.

One anecdote I remember well, happened on the Monday after graduation, when the school year was over. I was in my office doing paperwork, when in came an irate twenty-something first-year English teacher who had been fired because she had poor rapport with the kids and lacked classroom management. At first, I was surprised to see her in the building since school was over. When I calmed her down, she reported to me that one of the seniors had just squirted her with a water pistol and had called her an "old bitch." I told her she wasn't old and that I no longer had authority over the student. Besides, he had left the building. She left my office madder than when she came in. My secretary had overheard the conversation and came over to me laughing. She said she couldn't believe I that I had said, "You're not old." Probably my best spontaneous line ever!

The role of assistant principal is very different from that of the principal. Most of the job description is to take care of the nuts and bolts of the operation and whatever else the principal doesn't want to do, which includes being the one responsible for fire drills; assemblies; getting substitute teachers; patrolling the halls, bus platform, and parking lot; and supervising extracurricular events (games, dance, etc.). Teachers were paid for supervising extracurricular events, but the assistant principal didn't.

The assistant principal's primary function was to take care of discipline referrals. This would wear you down. High school students seem programmed to break the rules and push the envelope further each day. Occasionally you would feel professional when you observed (evaluated) a teacher. The vice principal title should really read the principal in charge of vice. Fortunately for me, my experience was limited to one year.

My first year in administration was not what I expected. When I was working as a teacher of science, I never felt the faculty as a whole disliked the principal or assistant principal—tolerated perhaps. I found a large segment of the high school faculty very anti-administration, whether it was at the district, state, or building level. Maybe it was a sign of the civil unrest going on in our society at the time. To share some examples, administration memos were marked, graded, and corrected (usually by English teachers) and left on the faculty lunchroom tables. Memos from the district office, even complimentary ones, were put on the bulletin board, and used as dart targets. If one of the three building administrators (principal and two assistants) didn't live up to what teachers wanted to have done to a student, we were bad-mouthed and dragged over their collective ire.

My worst experience, since I was trying my hardest to be a strict disciplinarian, was to find a faculty protest letter on the men's room door in the teachers' lunchroom enumerating their complaints about how bad the school was being run and how horrible discipline was. It was like reading Martin Luther's ninety-five theses against the Roman Catholic Church. It really hurt!

You could not do enough to support teachers, including covering a class, letting them leave early, or other favors. But it didn't work in reverse. Let one rumor of discontent start, and within one hour the whole faculty (groupthink) was in on it. I often felt like they were more emotional than intellectual. They seemed to love to bitch, moan, and scapegoat. Thank God for the holiday weeks off and the summer break. I did find however, the day-to-day challenges, the unexpected, solving problems, more challenging than the routine of the classroom, and that was my saving grace.

Beginnings of Disillusionment

Experiencing Burn-Out and
Midlife Crisis at Home and Work
1967 – 1980

Principal-South Sea Middle School 1975

Everybody at some point is going to have adversity. I think if we don't learn from that, then it was just a penalty. But if you use it, then it becomes tuition.

- Dr. Phil McGraw

Once you accept yourself, you can give yourself help that is little short of miraculous.

- Maxell Maltz

Having worked as an assistant principal for only one year, I was surprised that the superintendent, Dr. L asked me to become the principal of the South Sea Middle School for the 1967-1968 school year. The salary was $13,000 a year (the same I was paid the year before as an assistant).

Although only thirty-one years old, but somewhat brave and confident, I embarked on my principalship. I did not have an assistant, which made it particularly tough. There were many days when I felt like I was the only one in the building. I understood the progressive philosophy of Dr. L, and I was a firm believer in the emerging middle school mission to focus on the needs of early adolescents and not be a traditional junior high school where the emphasis was more on academics than total growth.

Team teaching was the instructional strategy that most middle schools utilized. It was the way the teachers could coordinate and integrate instruction. It also provided more flexibility and control of time by the teachers. I soon found out that the old guard, veteran teachers wanted nothing to do with team teaching. Their attempts to sabotage the program were many, including telling parents it was "soft" and "doesn't work."

Fortunately for me, with the support of Dr. L and the school board, that was the direction we were going. So over the next two years, the unhappy older, tenured teachers were transferred or requested transfers to the high school, where they belonged. After the majority of teachers became student rather than content oriented, the acceptance and enthusiasm toward team teaching and the middle school mission grew.

Perhaps the hardest job in middle school education is to have a faculty that is *trained for,* and *enjoys* working with early adolescents. Teachers tend to be secondary or elementary oriented, but what is needed, is a blend of both. The teacher's certification requirements and college education programs though, train for one or the other, (fortunately, this is changing now).

I can't overstate how important and efficient secretaries are. I could never type that fast, while being interrupted by a phone call or staff member and still stay task oriented. They play very significant roles in the smooth running of a school office, especially given their ability to listen to different constituents (teachers, students, parents, etc.) calmly and effectively. They insulate the administrator from many problems with their great human relations skills. They serve a significant aspect of a schools public relations program. Because of this, I never liked classifying them as *nonprofessional* staff. They were often more professional then the so-called professional staff. Secretaries and custodians were referred to as the *operational staff.* Thank God the vast majority of the operational staff are professionals in their own jobs and truly make the school district function twenty-four/seven.

I was blessed to have a personal secretary that was truly a pro. Her name was Ellie. Without a good secretary, a principal (or any boss) and especially a young rookie principal, would be lost. I'll never forget advice she gave me. At the time, my oldest son, Brian, was attending South Sea as an eighth grader. It was tough on him having his dad as principal. Brian used to give me feedback that the students thought I was very stern and never smiled. So I decided to improve my image and smile more. I was doing this for about two weeks. Ellie was in my office taking dictation (her nickname for me was Mr. Memo) when I braved asking her if she noticed if I was smiling more, trying to improve my public persona. She replied, "Well, Mr. Bennett, if you are, you better inform your face." So much for my changed demeanor.

Part of the function of a good secretary was to tell the truth. Truth hurts. Lack of truth hurts more, though. It helps to get feedback when you need it. God bless all the wonderful professionals that make up school operational staffs. They are the original multitasking ones who were competent and able to stay focused on what was important.

Ellie was most comforting and helpful when my mother passed away from stomach cancer in December 1967. She had been in Mineola Hospital for four months and was down to ninety pounds. I was grateful God took her from her suffering. She tried her best to be Mom and Dad to me. She also worked low-paying jobs to keep the family going, and I admired her for that.

During my first year at South Sea, I had to do a crisis intervention in the second floor girl's room. The female teacher who was on corridor duty near the main stairs summoned me. A girl had just informed her that another girl was in one of the toilet stalls with a knife and was trying to slash her wrists. I ran up to the second floor and sent the teacher into the girl's room to alert any other students to leave because I needed to enter right away. Fortunately, no one else was in the room, so I went right in.

I found Maria, an eighth-grade girl, sitting in a toilet stall up on the windowsill with her back firmly pressing on the large glass windowpane. She had a hunting knife in her right hand and appeared to be trying to slash her left wrist. Fortunately, the knife was very dull, and she hadn't succeeded. As I tried to communicate with Maria, standing in front of the stall, I was more worried about her falling backwards out through the large window. After much worry and anxiety on my part, I was finally able to encourage her to hand me the knife. It took me several more minutes to get her to come down off the windowsill. I called for one of our school psychologists to immediately assess her condition. I also called her mother to inform her of the severity of this act and the need for therapy for Maria and possibly the family. It seemed to work out, as Maria's attitude improved, and there were no more attempts at taking her life. A very scary memory, even now.

About two weeks into the school year, roughly fifteen minutes after the buses left at dismissal, I received not only one, but two phone calls from parents who told me they saw a student driving the school bus. Although my tendency was to think they were seeing things, since two parents reported the same incident, I decided I better go and check it out. My first phone call was to our assistant superintendent for business (who was in charge of bus transportation) to inform him of the parents allegations and that I was calling the bus company to request the driver return to school as soon as possible to explain to me why I received these calls. After getting permission from him to call, I spoke with the owner of the bus company. He informed me that he would have the bus driver return to talk to me, but that the drivers union contract called for the shop steward to be present and that he, too, wanted to be a witness to what the driver would say. So I called back the assistant superintendent to tell him to please join me at the conference later, which he did.

I'll never forget that scene. Bob and I were seated in my office and in comes a young male bus driver, the shop steward, and Mr. F., the owner of the bus company. After thanking them all for coming in to meet with me, I explained that I received two calls from parents that they allegedly saw a boy driving the bus.

Without batting an eye, the driver said, "It's true, damn right. I told this pain in the ass to drive!"

Bob and I looked at each other in disbelief. I said, "Tell me more...how could that happen?"

"Ever since school started this pain in the ass eighth grade boy would sit behind me every time he could. He told me I was a lousy driver and didn't know how to drive the bus. So, when he said it again when the kids were getting off the bus, I'd had it! I told him if you think you can drive better than me—you drive. So I got up, and we switched seats. The motor was running so all he had to do was work the transmission and clutch. I knew he wouldn't be able to. And sure enough, the bus bucked and stalled because he didn't give it enough gas. Since he forgot to close the door, it was easy for the parents who had been by the bus stop to look in and see why the bus jerked forward and stopped in the middle of the intersection. I guess that's why they called you. I fixed that S.O.B. eighth grader. He got to me, and I fixed him good. He'll never open his mouth again about my driving."

At this point, all other parties in the room looked at each other in embarrassment, before I could say anything, Mr. F. asked the bus driver and the shop steward to meet with him outside my office. Bob and I couldn't believe what we heard! After about five minutes, Mr. F. came back into my office without the driver and shop steward. He apologized to us but also explained that he could not take any other action against the driver since the union contract said there had to be three incidents before anything could be done, and this was the first problem with the driver. I responded that was his problem, but I could not let the parents see the driver on that bus tomorrow as they might think I had done nothing to follow up on their valid complaints. Mr. F. understood my public relations dilemma, and with Bob agreeing something had to be done for such a serious problem, he solved the situation by telling us he would transfer him to drive buses in another district tomorrow. That way it looked like we took action. While I couldn't believe more wasn't done to the driver, at least our immediate problem was addressed. I called back the parents to thank them for reporting the incident and that the driver wouldn't be driving that bus anymore. Unbelievable. Truth is stranger than fiction.

One day in January 1969, just after the last lunch period, one of the custodians came in to tell me the flag on the third floor stairwell railing had been set on fire (in '69 flag burning was in the media almost everyday). I immediately went with him to see the location and the flag, which did not totally burn. It tore me up to think one of our (my) students would do such a thing! But at the same time, the practice of bringing in the flag when it was raining and letting it dry on the stair railing was pretty dumb, especially in a middle school! I took the flag to my office and called in the head custodian to tell him to get another flag immediately and to never leave the flag on the railing again. (Talk about closing the barn door after the horse is gone!)

About half an hour after the incident was reported to me, I received a phone call from a reporter at the local newspaper (*L.I. Advance*) who wanted to know more about the "student demonstration" and "American flag burning" at the school. I asked him how he got the information and all he could tell me was that two of my female teachers had called him to report the disgrace. I explained that no one saw the incident, that it occurred between class periods, and that I was in the process of finding out who was late for class or got a corridor pass so I could find the culprit. I told him I could call him back when I had more information. It wasn't long before I narrowed it down to a ninth grade girl who just transferred into the school the day before from another district, who was classified as emotionally disturbed, and placed in special education. I suspended her, had her pay for a new flag, write a short essay on the meaning-significance of the American Flag, and how it should be treated.

I immediately sent a report to the superintendent explaining the facts and my actions, so he could prepare the school board for a possible reaction from the community. I also informed the faculty and staff about the incident, but didn't tell them who had called the Advance to report it! I then called the reporter, explaining what really happened, and that it was not a demonstration. Fortunately, when the Advance news brief appeared later that week, it stated the facts, my disciplinary actions, and was objectively written.

I soon got feedback from several teachers as to which two colleagues made the call. I predicted who they were since they were anti-Cliff Bennett. I never spoke to them about their actions since I had no real proof, and let the rest of the faculty censure them (I hoped). Other than my embarrassment and chagrin, nothing else much came of that incident. It really hurt though, to think that your own "professional" staff would create a public relations problem for their own school and community.

The college student protests of the Vietnam War in the late 60's reached the high schools around the country... although I thought our community would be too conservative to join the wave. How wrong I was.

Around 10:00 A.M. one October morning, I received a call from the high school principal, telling me that some students had pulled the fire alarm and that hundreds of students were marching towards the Village Hall, VFW building, and my school, all of which were right next to each other, to hold a protest against the war. I thanked him for alerting me, since it would take about thirty minutes for the students to arrive.

The first thing I did was to put all doors on back lock (which means they can only be opened from the inside). I then went down to the boiler room where the main switches were, including the fire alarm relay. I turned it off, so if a high school student (or one of mine) pulled the internal alarms, the fire alarm system would not work. Right after I did that, I sent out a brief memo to all teachers and staff alerting them to the imminent arrival of the protestors. In it, I informed them that all doors were on back lock, no students were to leave the building, for any reason, and that I had temporarily disconnected the fire alarm system, so if they sensed smoke or a fire, they must report it verbally, immediately to me or any custodian, and we would activate the fire alarm system, evacuate the building, and call the fire department.

In about thirty-five minutes, over 500 high school students were sitting on the lawns of the Village Hall, VFW Building, and the South Sea Middle School. Many had brought placards that echoed what they saw in the media: Peace Now, End the War, etc. Many students sat and made peace signs with their fingers. They encouraged our students to come out and join them, but we were able to keep our students on task. Police arrived and after an hour or so, the students started to disband and leave. There was no violence and no arrests.

After dismissal, I called the fire department to tell them that at 4:00 P.M. I was going to test the fire alarm system, and that if it went off, not to roll the trucks. I instructed my custodians (I had four in the building at that time) to each take a floor and if an alarm went off, to check all fire boxes to see if they had been pulled, and, to reset it. At exactly 4:00 P.M. I reset the main fire alarm relay in the boiler room. Immediately the alarm system went off (which I expected). After the custodians reported back to me, there had been three alarm boxes pulled, one on each of the second, third, and fourth floors. It kind of made my day; I would have loved to see the disappointment on the faces of those kids when the alarm didn't work. I was one step ahead of them—at least that day. Looking back on that challenging choice, I'm not sure it was the safest response. Fortunately, it worked. Thank God we didn't experience a real fire during the time the alarm system was off.

While you do tire of the role of disciplinarian that goes with being principal, especially when you have to call parents (which should always be the last resort—solve the problem with the student and/or teacher) or suspend a student, I learned to value getting to know the students. I think the key was to always accept the person but disapprove of the behavior. Remember that bad behavior does not make a bad child. Kids need role models, and need to experiment and blunder before they learn to do it right. I'm amazed how often one of my former students says hello to me and asks if I remember what they did and that I had suspended them. I would always treat each student with dignity, no matter how serious the offense. You overcome bad behavior with love, support, and optimism for the future. And a lecture on realizing the consequences of your choices. Think before you act.

Back in the 60's and 70's, it was not unusual for some parents to request you use corporal punishment on their child, as they, also, were often at wits' end. Depending on the boy, (I would never think of paddling a girl) and only *with* parental permission, would I administer it. I always had my assistant principal be a witness.

I always kept an anecdotal record of all my conferences with students referred for discipline. It was helpful in determining new approaches to affect change, especially for repeat offenders who invited challenging choices. Reviewing the record forced me to create different alternatives, because if I let my emotion override my mind, my inclination was to paddle the student, although I only used corporal punishment as the last resort. I knew from research the only person who benefited from corporal punishment was the giver, not the receiver. The act of physically striking another person helps dissipate your anger and frustration, as well as giving a false sense of control. There is no real benefit or change in attitude in the person receiving punishment, especially if it was painful or unjustified.

However, some teachers relied on the use and threat of power or physical punishment to maintain classroom management. It was sad to see them use techniques of fear to keep control. Instead of learning how to engage students through positive group dynamics, interesting challenging lessons, and gaining rapport and respect, they relied solely on amplifying their ego.

Another challenging choice for repeat offenders was my option of suspension. Although I did suspend students on occasion for serious behavior (fighting, insubordination, destruction of property, etc) for periods of three to five days, I did not think it was effective. In a sense, it was giving the student a vacation from school, albeit they still had to make up the lessons and homework they missed. Also, it could be problematic for parent(s), if they both worked.

Yet, for some students who were hard to enlighten, and to demonstrate the need to behave properly to all students, out of school suspension had it's place. I preferred to use in-school suspension whenever possible. It was more practical and effective.

No matter which choices you made, it always seemed that you were damned if you did, and damned if you didn't. Depending on the student, some teachers would give me feedback I was either too strong or weak in my punishment. Or, I received a memo from the superintendent that my monthly suspension report showed too many students were being suspended and requesting a memo due the next day on why and what I was planning to do to minimize future suspensions.

Another issue (concern) I had to prevent was students being pushed into special education just because they were different or difficult. Who owns the problem—the student or one teacher's attitude or lack of effective instruction? Most children, even problematic ones, just need more love, patience, practice, acceptance, and understanding to succeed.

It often felt like you couldn't win, no matter how much thought you put into the outcomes of your decision. I also learned not to decide - is to decide. Sometimes it was better to suspend judgment and make the decision at a later time, when you have more perspective. It also helped to grow thick skin, but not rabbit ears.

Some kids find misbehaving as the only way to be stroked by their parents, although it's negative attention. Better to be punished than not to be recognized at all. This pattern continues in school for many students.

Corporal punishment was banned in our school district by a change in school board policy in 1976. I was glad of it, as some teachers still relied on it as their power source. Students did not take advantage of this change, as I predicted. True discipline or control must come from within. Students learn this by introspection and learning to *think* before they act and of *consequences* for them and their parents.

Also, most parents in the 80's shifted to protecting their child and defending them, whether right or wrong. You would pray parents would accept their responsibility to help you affect needed changes in behavior and attitude, especially in a school social setting. The emphasis on the me generation had taken root. We had started to live in a culture of narcissism— a *"me"* society, rather than an "us" society.

It became tradition at the South Sea Middle School, to take overnight (two nights) field trips; the seventh grade went to Washington, DC, and the eighth graders to Boston. Both were very tiring to the staff, as we were up all night monitoring the behavior in the rooms and keeping the lid on things. I'll always remember one Boston trip I chaperoned.

We had contracted with a reputable bus company that we used before without problem. We always tipped the drivers well and expected good, reliable service, which we received. However, this one time, when the buses arrived at 6:00 A.M., I was informed that the bus company had to subcontract for one of the buses as one of their buses was in the garage. After waiting a half hour for the last bus, I almost was going to tell the other four buses to leave, but I wanted us to stay as a caravan. Finally, the subcontracted bus arrived. I could not believe my eyes! While it was a motor coach, it was painted bright purple and emblazoned on the sides of it in large printing was, First Church Tabernacle of Jesus Christ, Holy Redeemer and Savior, Newark, NJ. I was grateful the parents had left already, having dropped off their children at 5:45 A.M., so they couldn't see this eggplant with wheels. How could I explain the separation of church and state? Having no alternative, we climbed aboard. I introduced myself to the bus driver, a young Afro-American man who introduced himself to me as the "Baby Maker." Just what I needed to hear.

So our caravan started out forty-five minutes later than expected, but we were on the road again. But not for long. We made it to Commack Road on the Long Island Expressway, which is about fifteen miles from school, when the bus driver informed me he was out of fuel and wanted to know if I had any money or a credit card to pay for diesel fuel. I told him I had a credit card he could use, and we fueled up just off the L.I.E. Great start! After we got back on the L.I.E to rejoin the other buses, he would C.B. radio the other bus drivers every half hour (throughout the trip) with his C.B. handle, "This is the "Baby Maker"...come in." I really needed this; it went so well with the name on the bus.

To add insult to injury, on the way home, in Connecticut, our bus got a flat tire. "Baby Maker" informed me he had no spare, but he knew where there is a tire company that can fix us up quick. "You still got that credit card?" he asked. Needless to say, it was the last time we used that bus company, but they did reimburse me for the cost of the fuel and the tire.

Thank God we got back in the dark of the night, and it was hard to read what was written on the bus, (or parents didn't notice). This incident led to a new school board policy on checking out the safety record, insurance, equipment, etc. of all contracted buses, especially those used for field trips, so there was a silver lining.

My daughter Susan was born on June 28, 1970. We now had four wonderful children—two boys and two girls. The perfect family, it seemed at the time.

During the 70's, the middle school philosophy flourished, as did our educational programs. We had team teaching, an activity period built into the school day, and comprehensive intramurals for the boys and girls (homeroom vs. homeroom by grade level). The kids loved coming to school. One of our innovations was to do away with the stereotype of boys taking industrial arts and the girls, home economics. Since the concept of androgyny was emerging in our society, we blended the best of both programs, calling it home arts. Classes were coed, still taught by the I.A. and home ec. teachers. The seventh and eighth graders really liked the program, as did the teachers since we developed a schedule where physical education and home arts classes had a double period on alternate days, allowing for more time for activities.

However, one parent of an eighth grade boy (Tony) did not. He called me to request his son be taken out of the program since it was making him into a "girl." I tried my best to explain the philosophy behind the coed classes, but he didn't want to hear it. We were making a "woman" out of his man. So I called him to come into school to meet with me, visit the class, confer with the teacher, (Debra DeBeno), and then decide. He agreed to come in the next morning at 9:00 A.M.

When he entered my office, he was very emotional. I never had a parent bang his fist on my desk before, so I let him ventilate, to blow off some steam, before talking with him. After ten minutes, he calmed down. So I asked him if he wanted to observe the home arts class that his son was in. "Absolutely not! Get my son out of there!" I was able, however, to get him to at least meet with the teacher, hoping she could convince him the program was sound and would not "sissify" his son.

I had clued Debra in to Mr. T's concerns the day before. I was confident she and I could convince him to let Tony stay. Little did I know how powerful his male/female paradigms and stereotypes were. We soon found out.

I buzzed my secretary and asked her to get a teacher that was free to cover Debbie's class so she could come to the office to meet with Mr. T and me. Within a few minutes, Debra knocked on my door. Fortunately, Mr. T had calmed down, and I felt he would listen. Further, since Debbie was attractive, enthusiastic, and a great teacher, she would win the day. How wrong I was.

Deborah entered my office, dressed very professionally. I introduced them to each other. I said, "Mr. T, this is Tony's home arts teacher, Ms. DeBeno."

"Mr. Beno!" "Mr. Beno!" Mr. T exclaimed. "You better get my kid out of this class. You got a goddamned transvestite teaching him!"

Debbie looked at me, and I realized she was equally dumbfounded. It was obvious this meeting was going no place, and I thought I was dealing with a lunatic. So I dismissed Debbie and asked Mr. T to stay, so we could talk further (if possible). Then it struck me why he heard "Ms. DeBeno" as "Mr. Beno." His rigid mindset blended "Ms. De" to become "Mr." He couldn't hear the Ms. DeBeno as separate parts, or even use his eyes to check out his ears!

Since it was obvious to me I wasn't going to be able to persuade Mr. T to let Tony stay in the class, I reluctantly took him out, telling Mr. T he would have to study the content of the course in the library by himself, since I had no other elective for him. He agreed. This arrangement lasted for just two weeks. I received a phone call from Mr. T requesting I put Tony back in that "transvestite's" class because he hated being by himself in the library. The power of peer pressure... and a closed mind.

During the 1960's and early 1970's, when the school district was growing, we actually had to recruit teachers by visiting college campuses and announcing interview sites at hotels in cities throughout the Eastern Seaboard. One very memorable experience occurred during a recruiting trip in the winter of 1971 to upstate New York with my dear friend John, one of the elementary principals.

After we were finished interviewing on a cold Tuesday at Ithaca College, we were heading for the district's station wagon, which we were given for these assignments. John and I decided to ask two coeds who were walking toward us to suggest a neat place near by to have dinner and if possible, some fun or entertainment on a Tuesday night in snowy, cold Ithaca. Without hesitating, they both said, "You have to go to the Clover Club. It's the only cool place open around here on Tuesday night." After getting directions, south of Ithaca about ten miles, we thanked them and returned to our motel.

We arrived at the Clover Club around 7:00 P.M. It was easy to find, being the only building around for several miles. There were only three cars in the large parking lot in front of the building. This did not inspire confidence in the quality of the restaurant. However, we had been assured this was the "best and only cool place in town on Tuesday evening" so we said, why not?

Upon entering the Clover Club, we saw one guy playing billiards at the only pool table, directly in the front of the bar, where the bartender, tightly wrapped in a white apron like an Egyptian mummy, stood on duty. That was it, for a large restaurant, at 7:10 p.m. Not a great endorsement. However, we weren't about to go riding around to find another place, so we went up to the bar and asked the bartender if the kitchen was open. "Sure it's open," he said, "Want to see our menu?" Good start.

After having a draft beer, John and I asked the bartender where we should go to sit. There was a four-foot wall separating the bar-pool table area from the restaurant section, which had about fifteen tables, a platform with a jukebox on it, and a small dance floor in front of that. He said he would get the waitress to seat us.

"Jane" he screamed. "Come here." "After you guys have dinner, do you want to buy a ticket to our 9:00 P.M. show?" he asked, as Jane came out from the swinging kitchen doors.

"What kind of a show?" I asked.

"Dancing," the bartender replied.

"Sure," we both said.

"Okay. That'll be two dollars each for admission, and if you want to stay for the 11:00 P.M. show, I'll stamp the back of your hand, so you won't have to pay again."

Wow, I thought to myself, although no one else had come into the Clover Club since John and I arrived, the crowd probably came closer to show time. So John and I paid the bartender the entertainment fee and had our hands stamped in case the "show" was good, and we felt like staying for the last performance.

Jane now escorted us to the restaurant side of the club. "Sit where you'd like, but you may want to take a table in the middle near the dance floor, to see the show better."

We took her advice. Forget the dinner—bring on the show! Perhaps the coeds gave us good advice after all! Jane was around forty, pleasant looking, but shy. She took our orders, and the food wasn't bad. By the time we finished dinner, it was almost 9:00 P.M. No one else had come into the Clover Club. So John and I just stayed where we were seated, since we were really lucky to get the best seats in the house.

At 9:00 P.M. on the dot, the bartender stood up on a platform behind the bar, and bellowed out to the three customers (John, the guy still playing pool by himself, and me), "Ladies and Gentlemen, welcome to the Clover Club. It's time for our early show. Please proceed to the table area now!" John and I couldn't help but laugh, given the absurdity of the situation. We now couldn't wait for the show. Which turned out to be Jane, our waitress. She came out of the kitchen doors dressed in the most outrageous dancing costume I ever saw. I think she made it of old curtains. It had numerous layers, and I guess it was supposed to look Spanish, as she had castanets in the palms of both hands. She made her way to the platform where she was joined by the bartender. "Ladies and Gentlemen, the Clover Club is proud to present Jane, for your enjoyment!" They made quite a pair! After introducing Jane to the audience (just John and I, you could hear the other patron playing pool), the bartender returned to the bar.

Jane just stood there, looking across the club at the bartender. After a couple of minutes of awkward standing, wondering when the music would start, finally, Jane blurted out to the bartender, "For God sakes, Frank, put some quarters in the machine. You forgot to put in money. How the hell am I supposed to dance?" John and I lost it. We couldn't help but crack up at this Broadway musical. Frank came over, put in a few quarters (he took from the cash register), muttered something under his breath, and returned to the bar. Jane was now busy pushing in her dance music for the 9:10 P.M.

show. I wondered if she would choose different records or wear a different costume for the 11:00 P.M. performance?

The Jukebox started, Jane got off the platform and started swirling around the room clicking the castanets as she swayed back and forth, trying to keep rhythm with the music. Since we were the only audience, Jane paid the most attention to our table. She seemed to have the hots for John, as she kept bending over in front of him and brushing up against him as she danced. I got the cold shoulder but was laughing, so I deserved it; I had never seen such a funny sight. After four forty-fives played, Jane bowed, accepted our applause, and retired to the kitchen.

John and I decided we had to stay for the 11:00 P.M. show! So we went back to the bar and had a couple of beers to kill time. No one else came into the Clover Club. The pool player left around 10:30 P.M. John and I were the only ones there at 11:00 P.M. Suddenly, the bartender blurted out, "Ladies and Gentlemen, it's time for the 11:00 P.M. show. Please proceed to the table area now." So John and I got up and headed for our table. We didn't go ten feet when the bartender asked us if we paid for the show. We were flabbergasted! Although we assured him we had paid, he told us to come to the entrance area by the restaurant side opening, and on a small table, put our hands under the ultraviolet light to show the stamps on the back of our hands. We passed the test! We hadn't changed! And we didn't have to pay admission!

The 11:00 show went more smoothly than the 9:00. After Frank got the attention of the "ladies and gentlemen" in the room, he remembered to deposit four quarters so Jane could start her routine right away. She wore the same ludicrous outfit, complete with castanets. But she chose different songs; it's just too bad there was no one else there to witness the act. Between Frank and Jane, it was quite a show. I often wonder if the Clover Club is still there, who's on the bill, and if they draw bigger crowds on Tuesday nights in the winter.

Way back in the 70's, we could still have dress codes. One day around fifth period (12:05 P.M.), a ninth grade girl was sent to the office with a referral stating her clothing was interfering with the teaching-learning process. She was mature for her age and wearing a brown open-net pullover that exposed more than it covered. I wondered two things: the teacher that sent her down was a male in his 30s—was it affecting him or the class? 2. She must have had four female teachers before him who didn't notice her nipples almost coming out of the net mesh. I tried not to look at her. I had to find a solution.

My decision, since she lived just one block from school was to let her go home, put on something more appropriate, and come back. She (like many other minority students) did not have a phone at home. I knew her mother and felt she would agree with me. Sure enough, in ten minutes, she was back in the main office asking to see me. When she came into my office, I couldn't believe my eyes. She was wearing the same brown mesh pull over except she had on a light purple satin bra that was more distracting than before! I asked if she had anything else at home to wear, but she said "No." Fortunately for the two of us, I had a separate conference room next to my office where she did her assignments for the remainder of the day. Worked. She dressed better in the future.

As principal of a secondary school, you never know what's going to happen minute to minute, or from inside or outside the building. A classic example is when two federal agents (FBI and Treasury) showed up in the main office unannounced. They entered my office and showed their impressive credentials. Seems the problem they were investigating was that counterfeit quarters were showing up in the Sunday mass pew collections in the Catholic Church directly across the street from our school.

When I inquired what this had to do with me or our school, I was told the church officials were convinced the counterfeit coins were being put in the collection plate by middle school age boys, and they wanted to know if we offered industrial arts that included metal shop, specifically how to use a foundry (casting with molten metal). Yes, we did have that as part of our curriculum. They asked if we could go to the shop and talk with the industrial arts teacher, which of course, we did. We found that the unit on metal casting was taught the previous month and students learned how to make impressions of coins in the fine sand as a demonstration.

Well, it didn't' take long for Mr. J., our industrial arts teacher, and me to narrow down the usual list of suspects (eighth graders) that would play around and make imitation quarters on their own. By the way, the agents brought a few, and they looked authentic at first glance. The bank where they were deposited didn't appreciate the slugs, and reported it to the church. Between the two, it now became an offense worthy of investigating.

I asked the federal agents to give me two days, so I could do my detective work and would call them when I was sure who the culprits were. Only took me an hour or two. I went over the class lists and developed my cast of possible perpetrators. I interrogated the top four, who from experience might try such mischief. I interviewed them separately, but called two down together, having one wait in the outer office while I spoke with the other. I missed my first hunch, but the second dynamic duo admitted their "crime." I used the strategy of "good cop-bad cop" by playing both roles, and it worked. I explained this was a serious offense, and I would have to contact their parents, which I did. They didn't seem surprised.

When I called the federal agents, they wanted to come to school to arrest the boys. I talked them out of this course of action, explaining I had already informed their parents, would suspend the boys from school for a day, and that they had to make a donation to the Catholic Church for double the amount of quarters they had given in the collections. I assured them that the foundry in the metal shop would only be used with *strict* teacher supervision in the future. They agreed and thanked me for cooperating. That was a real triple whammy—the Catholic Church, FBI, and the Treasury Department! Usually though, by touching all the bases smoothly, these unexpected dilemmas would disappear. An interesting dilemma.

I enjoyed my thirteen years as principal at South Sea. I learned many lessons and had my philosophy of human relations affirmed. My first lesson was to expect and accept the diversity of the faculty. While you wished everyone liked you and embraced your philosophy of education, each teacher brings his or her own basket to the picnic. You had to learn to become a symphony conductor that needs all the diverse instruments and skills of all the musicians. It's also very difficult to be a prophet in your own community.

While I hated the adversarial relationship and confrontational style of some teachers (and other staff members), the unions promoted this practice. Once a month, whether there was a need to or not, the union representatives met with you to file their concerns, complaints, and observations. What made it difficult was you never felt we were in the same boat.

You seldom received a thank you, compliment, or understanding for your set of problems. It seemed the faculty wanted the school to function with no discipline problems or other hurdles (Shangri La). I'm convinced that just as a society gets the crime rate it deserves, so does a school get the behavior and achievement it gets from the community it services (and the attitude of the faculty toward their students). Looking back, I had almost as many problems with a few teachers as with students and parents. But, that goes with the ranch and role of a secondary principal.

Fortunately, in both the high school and South Sea, there was a majority of open-minded, mature, and friendly teachers who gave support when you needed it. You knew the negative feedback was emotional "group-think" by teachers who view their roles as a job, not a profession.

I knew from my elementary school colleagues, that the mindset of elementary teachers was different from secondary teachers, who focus more on subject matter content. Elementary teachers are predominately female, child oriented, parent oriented, and not so union minded. They are very committed to coming into school a week before school opens to decorate and ready their classroom, and stay late to prepare for the next day. Speaking generally, they seemed to really enjoy their work.

I was also made aware of how different the behavior of elementary students was: compliant, listened well, and respectful. A whole different world. A very pleasant environment to be in. I had to choose the struggles of adolescence! But it was very challenging and rewarding in it's own way. Middle school age children are open, fun loving, and enthusiastic. They're fun if you know how to bond with them.

Most teachers meant well and really cared about kids. They did their job and appreciated you doing yours. But a vocal minority were unhappy campers. I often wondered if they ever attended college or really had an earned degree(s). They wanted their classroom to be utopia and kids never to change. Their attitude toward the total school was myopic. Administrators refer to such gripers as suffering from *classroom mentality*: the inability to see the school, school system, or community as a dynamic, constantly changing flux. These teachers just loved to complain and bitch. They seemed to expect you to be able to hold on to the past and keep things from changing. Even parents were viewed as pains in the ass. Their classroom was their kingdom. This group never could see their rigidity and anger. I felt sorry for them. They probably felt sorry for me.

Perhaps this group of unhappy campers were reflecting the results of burnout. This is a common experience for anyone serving in the people professions like; teachers, police officers, nurses, counselors, store clerks, etc., who constantly deal with the public and their constant complaints. Add to this the perception that your job requirements and restrictions (true of teaching and school administration) keep expanding each year while the rewards and job satisfactions diminish. This negative vortex puts you into a grave you keep digging with your own empty protests. Few see they need to stop making a grave with no ends.

What's needed is to put some fire back into your heart and soul. Only you can balance your life. Are you living to work, or working to live? What you focus on will expand. The glass looks emptier each day and increases your pessimism and bitterness toward the world. Balance work with play, fun, and relaxation. Seek life's gifts in many places. Work is work. Keep life in perspective.

While dealing with teachers was difficult at times (especially the prima donnas), you also had to walk a tightrope with the expectations of the superintendent and other district office administrators. You would do your best to be perfect for the image that central office wanted to create, but no matter how hard you tried, your evaluations and feedback always showed shortcomings. Seldom did you get a compliment, but no complaint, no matter how small or unfounded, was ever withheld. You really had to develop thick skin and just work to enjoy the problem solving and relationships with the kids, staff, and parents. If you were other directed, you'd never make it. Being a school administrator is a very complex and lonely job. You have to create your own psychic rewards and just know you are doing a good job despite your perception of feedback you're not.

Teachers didn't seem to realize that the education laws that benefited (protected) them, also had a spin-off effect on the way administrators had to evaluate them. None of us like to receive a negative written evaluation. We all prefer to learn we're doing fine and appreciated. But there exists a definite line that must be drawn in ink and maintained in a paper trail when there is objective criteria that part of a teachers performance needs improvement, for example, classroom management: discipline, rapport with students, quality and quantity of tests, etc.

I remember attending many administrative workshops led by attorneys and labor specialists that would demonstrate examples of poorly written "negative" evaluations, usually just damning with faint praise. We were constantly being reminded (and evaluated) on how specific and strong our written criticism had to be. This practice didn't sit well with the recipients of a negative evaluation. We were supposed to be colleagues and friends. It was very difficult to have a teacher understand I had a job to do, and I was being evaluated by my evaluations—how would they hold up in a court of law or a 3020-A tenure removal hearing?

It was difficult to be in this double bind, win-lose battle. Building administrators have to maintain a cordial relationship with the staff to keep the ship running primarily keeping staff, students, and parents happy campers. But we also have to wear the badge of deputy sheriff and please the superintendent of schools, other district office administrators, who are our bosses. They too, are in a double bind, trying to please the school board, P.T.A.s, state education officials, teachers, administrators, and staff. Not an easy job.

School districts have two levels of organization: formal (administration, school board, education law, teacher unions) and informal (staff and faculty, individually and collectively). At the building level, where the principal has day-to-day contact with teachers and needs their cooperation and support, you have to walk a tightrope to balance what the formal organization expects and what the informal organization is willing to do. The informal group can be particularly strong if they have a history of longevity, control, and an administrator who wanted the comfort of friends rather than just colleagues. I inherited a faculty that had a critical mass composed of local community residents with a history of emotional bonding, including the previous principal, who was a fellow faculty member. There was much groupthink I had to overcome.

One of the stress management techniques I developed during my years at South Sea was to get involved with sports officiating. I started out with football and then lacrosse, and I loved it so much that I then did some girls' sports, basketball, field hockey, and softball. I enjoyed every minute of it. You would work a game with someone from a different occupation, and you didn't talk shop! Between understanding the rules and the physical exercise, you also had to learn new mechanics of covering the playing field. I always felt more involved in the game I was refereeing than when I played a sport as a member of a team. You were always involved. I loved officiating! Especially making a final decision! It was like being a cop. When you blew your whistle, it was actually heard and obeyed!

Fortunately for me, realizing I needed more stress management skills and self-understanding (introspection rather than being outer oriented), I attended a seminar that really helped me better accept my work. The key concept, which I've applied daily since I learned it through today, is the "Richter Scale of Stress". This is an application of the geophysics principles of the energy released by an earthquake. In the Richter scale, for example, 4.5 is the threshold of physical damage to buildings.

Most distress is brought about by our own perception (interpretations) of external events. One to three on the Richter Scale of Stress might be; being late, spilling coffee, etc; four to six, a headache, an argument, etc. While seven to ten would be what really presses our buttons, someone talking on the cell phone instead of paying the cashier. Waiting on a long line for an item to be told they're all out, etc. What the Richter scale teaches us is that there are really few real tens, death of a loved one, divorce, your house burns down, etc. You can probably count them on one hand. But what we do through cognitive distortion (a.k.a. magnification) is we transform a one to three into a seven to ten. So the point is, to control your reactions to mostly neutral events and keep them where they belong. Remember,.... what you focus on,....EXPANDS. Avoid "stinkin thinkin" - mind farts.

This enabled me to be more objective (controlled subjectivity) about the realities in school. I could focus more on the positives, the music groups performing, our sports teams, the good things the student government did for the school and community, celebrating academic success, etc. To paraphrase Pogo, I have met the enemy, and it is I. What you focus on,....EXPANDS.

Doing something positive was helpful for me. I was invited to join the local Rotary Club (most administrators were in service clubs). This was rewarding personally and professionally. I had a chance to network with the other business men and professionals enjoying the chance to experience more positive and different viewpoints. I became president of the

Rotary Club in 1973. I value every minute of my thirty years as a Rotarian. Service Above Self, the motto of Rotary, benefits you as well as others.

At the close of the 1976-1977 school year, I was informed of teachers and staff that were being transferred to South Sea from the other two middle schools. Musical chairs was a favorite game of our superintendent for both teachers and administrators. Thank God for me, this round of transfers changed my life.

My school nurse was retiring, so I was sent another from the Eagle Elementary School, Judy K. When we met the last week of school in June, I was struck by her beauty. I found her relaxed, sincere, and deep. I couldn't wait for September to come, so I could get to know Judy better. I needed change. As I entered my forties, I began to realize I was more disillusioned with my marriage and school administration. I found both to be unrewarding, stressful, and draining.

My roles as husband and principal were missing something. Feelings of not being appreciated and respected became stronger. My fantasies about the positive expectations of marriage and being a principal were being tempered by reality. I was probably my own worst enemy since I'm an idealist and too sensitive.

I was living in a four-bedroom, two and one-half bath large colonial, complete with in-ground swimming pool on a cul-de-sac 500 feet from Great South Bay, in a well to do section in South Bayport. I was proud of my tenaciousness in buying it, overcoming Geri's concerns. She didn't seem to like moving from Nassau to Suffolk County, or my dream house in Bayport, or some of my colleague-friends. My pride in going from that Mineola apartment to my home in Bayport faded rapidly. Ever been on vacation with someone who didn't want to be? Something was missing, but I didn't know what it was. Looking back, it was like the empty feeling you understand when you listen to Peggy Lee's pensive song "Is that all there is?" My positive illusions had changed from negative, empty experiences of reality.

My role as principal was also taking its toll. No matter how much you gave, it seemed like it was never enough. I missed the daily dynamics and fun of being in the classroom teaching science. All I did now was chase the "bad" kids and deal with everyone else's problems and frustrations. I found little joy at work anymore. My expectations of the job did not match the realities. There were few rewards. The hole in my heart I was making was getting bigger and bigger. I was running on empty.

First the marriage. Understand this is only my side of the equation, my perceptions, and projections. You would have to balance my take with how my wife, Geri, felt about and saw my interactions with her and the four children.

Our start in marriage was shaky. We had our first child, Brian, nine months and one day (thank God) after we were married. It was a difficult delivery for Geri (she needed surgery to open the birth canal). I felt we were emotionally different after Brian's birth. I began to see changes in our personalities. We were both too young (twenty-two and twenty-three) to start a family. Our own maturation process of growing into secure individuals was stunted. Having a child was like culture shock. The freedom was gone. New responsibilities, obligations, and duties demanded your time and attention. It was like being in a ten-foot rowboat with a one-hundred-pound anchor.

Geri didn't have time to stay in her role as an elementary teacher. She had to stop working in 1960, as she was pregnant with Brian. It was an abrupt adjustment, to switch to role of mother. I was working on my master's degree part time at Hofstra, and soon found the need to get an extra job to meet expenses since we didn't have Geri's income. I'm not sure we were ready for so much responsibility, being locked into new roles without growing as mature individuals or as a secure married couple. We were not ready or ripe. Case of arrested development and fulfillment. We both had to adapt to our new obligations and become other oriented. We missed time to find ourselves in our careers and as new adults, away from the security of college life. We became interdependent before we were independent and sure of who we were as individuals.

Within two years of being married, I finished my master's degree at Hofstra University and was proud of my academic achievements. I was asked by two professors I had taken courses with (education and geology) to teach as an adjunct in both departments. I was very proud of this and still am. I looked forward to going to my master's graduation and hoped Geri would attend the ceremony with me. She did not. Instead, she went for a Sunday ride with her mother and father because they all thought it was a waste of time to go. That hurt. The first of many emotional withdrawals from our joint account.

I loved my children dearly, but I needed more than my father role at home. I was father all day, five days a week for ten months to 900 teenagers, many with little or any positive influence. On the other hand, Geri enjoyed her role as mother and found it fulfilling. We had become role locked in different ways. I loved my work, doing graduate studies, and teaching as an adjunct; we began to drift further and further apart. We needed to maintain and grow in our roles as individuals and lovers, which did not happen.

Our marital joint "bank account" had too many withdrawals with no deposits of any kind seen for the future. My own personal bank account was bankrupt. It was time to think about truly moving out of Williston Park, which I found myself back in, an emotional wasteland in my own home.

Something was missing. I had a beautiful wife, children, home, and good job. Yet I felt no fulfillment or joy in living. These facets of my life were not enough. I was my own worst enemy. The word *person* comes from the Latin word *persona* which means mask. We all wear three masks, public, personal, and private. The public mask is what everyone knows about you, the personal, what you are willing to share about yourself, and the private are your demons and dreams, which you keep secret. Part of my private world was an ideal dream of what romance, love, and marriage should be like. However, this was in conflict with my real world experience. My inner voice drove me to find and fulfill my dream and vision of happiness.

And, I finally felt it when I was with Judy. I truly felt accepted, respected, and appreciated. I was reborn when I was with her. There were only deposits of love and affection. My emotional bank account was again being filled, and I liked the feeling!

My hardest decision, ever, truly gut-wrenching, was to leave four children. But to save myself, despite the consequences, became my mission. Children become adults and leave home. I would give my children as much time and support as I could, and did.

I had developed too much scar tissue. We were no longer young college lovers. We (I) had not kept the fire burning. Although we both made genuine attempts to nurture our relationships, including marriage counseling, it didn't help. I initiated the divorce. Little did I know the price you have to pay. Going through the process of divorce was draining, emotionally and financially. Actually, the word *divorce* is a misnomer. You may be separated by a judge, but you are still emotionally attached through your roles as parents.

The American way of obtaining a divorce is very adversarial and deepens the chasm between spouses. The only ones that benefit are the lawyers. Margaret Mead had the right idea regarding an approach to marriage that would alleviate the emotional and financial pain. My lawyer said to me in the last trial conference, "We have agreed to pay two-thirds of your income for alimony and child support." _What we?_ Her concept was to enter into a five-year agreement that could be changed if one or both parties agreed to dissolve the relationship with no requirements for financial assistance other than equal disbursement of assets. In other words, a five-year renewable contract between "husband" and "wife." No lawyers or anguish needed if the parties decide to go their own ways. Win-win not win-lose or lose-lose.

It was a traumatic experience to go through the divorce. I felt very guilty leaving Geri with our children and even worse about leaving them without a full-time dad. But I knew

I wouldn't leave them entirely and that I could still show support and love. I wasn't divorcing them and made sure they knew that, as well as they were not the reason I was leaving. I felt bad for Geri. She was, and is, a good person. She was, and still is beautiful. Yet, I had reached a point where I had to save me, not the marriage. She wasn't experiencing the depth of despair that I was. So I made the most difficult challenging decision I've ever made, to get divorced, and try to save myself.

As to work, although I was proud to be a principal and loved the daily (sometimes hourly) unexpected challenges, it was tough to feel as if I were in a vise. The two sides of the vise were the superintendent's authoritarian style, which was very difficult to cope with, and the other side, a faculty that could never seem to be pleased. Students and parents were generally easy to work with and enjoyable. Yet no matter what you did in following up on a teacher's report of inappropriate student behavior, it was never enough.

There was seldom a faculty meeting held in my thirteen years as principal that the issue-problem of how bad discipline was and what was I going to do to improve school climate wasn't voiced. My response was usually to ask what could we do together to help students and parents? They didn't like ownership of the problem, which I knew. I just got tired of doing my best, and often thinking I overreacted or overstepped my usual attempts to reeducate students to make a better decision only to hear, one teacher(s) complain it wasn't enough! Who owns the problem? Not the main office. My office was seen as the police station. I found most teachers were reactive and not proactive when it came to problems they were having. Often I felt they contributed to the conflict but wouldn't dare tell them. The principal has to promote and maintain harmony, peace, and cooperation.

A building principal's job is a classic example of what's called middle management. You are smack in between teachers and parents who each want it their way and the pressure from district office (central administration) to do it their way—the correct image, politically neutral. You had to balance your decisions, so they pleased both sides; it was imperative to be a diplomat, as well as a policeman. I never could find "Solomon" pills, but always proceeded to benefit all parties involved. I learned how to walk a tightrope with a smile.

On a daily basis, it was a lose-lose proposition. Even though you were in a building with over 1,000 students, faculty, and staff, you often felt as if they weren't really there, and you were all alone. You had to constantly adjust, adapt, and effectively communicate with divergent needs. Within fifteen minutes, you had to respond to a burned-out head custodian complaining about his latest crisis, a prima-donna teacher asking for an unrealistic solution, an angry single parent, etc. You had to constantly switch hats and turn around your collar. I wished there was a Jiffy Lube I could go to once a week! I was now really caught in the vortex of both midlife crises and burnout. The expectations and daily requirements of work and marriage had exceeded the satisfactions. A double bind...and it was tightening.

One of the penalties of leadership is that you're damned if you do, and damned, if you don't. You need to develop thick skin and a durable ego. And you better have an adequate support system to keep on going, namely you, looking for the positives (which are there) and putting them into your emotional bank account. You cannot make your work role the sole purpose and meaning of your life. You need to nurture *yourself*, which is the most important role you have. Only you can keep the fire going in your heart and soul, through continuous mental and spiritual growth. Balance and renewal are keys to survival. To keep the light burning, you must put oil in your lantern, which I wasn't doing.

I had let the fire in my heart burn out. I was lost. By repressing my feelings and not processing them, I dug my own grave. My feelings of emptiness and loneliness were causing emotional stress and leading to a sense of extreme unhappiness. I felt like a bell without a clapper, broken, trapped and captive inside myself. I was living my total life in denial.

Years of being in a toxic marriage relationship had taken its toll. I was in an end-state condition caused by not taking control of my life circumstances, not being totally conscious of my real state of mind. By not seeking holistic self-fulfillment, ignoring my heart's song, and overvaluing compensatory roles, I was playing to rationalize my pain; I was not being responsible for my life.

Since I could not find respect, acceptance, appreciation, and encouragement at home, I sought them in other roles I was involved with in the community. However, those were all external involvement, providing little internal growth and challenges. I rationalized and overvalued these ancillary activities. I was placing my energy in social networking through memberships in the Rotary Club, Y.M.C.A., Patchogue-Medford Youth Services, and Brookhaven Memorial Hospital. Since I was getting few positive strokes at home and at work, I sought them elsewhere. While I enjoyed my involvement with these organizations, they could not plug the hole in my heart or comfort my soul.

To save myself, it became clear that I would have to apply leadership to my own life, to right the ship, to regain balance, and take control of my life. I had to find my true meaning and purpose. The main role that needed my attention and courage of conviction was that of being a unique individual entitled to the pursuit of happiness.

It was time to realize that teaching in-service courses – workshops, being involved in educational organizations, and publishing articles in professional journals was not filling the void in my life. I had to become centered, focused, and a whole person. To be cognizant of and act on the overall quality of my newfound self awareness, I knew deep inside I had to make the most challenging choice of my adult life, taking the risk of what would come from getting truly involved with Judy, since we worked together. I expected and we experienced negativity that came from others perceptions of our relationship. These would be caused by people protecting themselves, their comfort zones, and by projecting (attributing) to others their own faults, feelings, or attitudes. I (we) were not trying to please others or seek their approval. We knew what we were doing was right for us.

Thank God, the "lifeguard" in me saved me from drowning in self-pity. I (we) had lit a fire in my heart and soul that cast a light on a new life. The warmth from this newly created self-power was the catalyst I needed to bond with Judy and save myself. To fulfill and sing my heart's song. I accepted the challenge to boldly defy, to dare, to accept the ownership of my life, with all the costs involved.

My relationship with and salvation by Judy started slowly. I would talk with her in her office or mine about student medical problems. Soon we would share more personal information, and it was obvious to me we were very compatible. Soul mates. I found being listened to and respected very refreshing. We met for coffee at her apartment a few times, and I couldn't wait for my brief visits with her. We fell in love and the rest is history. Hardest decision of my life but the best. I was feeling alive again. Life now had meaning and purpose again. (See my poems "Mystical Magician" and "What I'd Give to Share This Feeling!" (pp. 151 + 165), that express my emotional state. They were written within weeks of being with Judy! I hadn't written a poem since college (1955-59). We were married July 19, 1980 and celebrated our thirtieth anniversary in 2010. Judy has accepted my four children (and they her) as well as supporting me in my roles as father and grandfather.

Fortunately for me, throughout the years since leaving home, my four children and I have maintained a close relationship. I'm so proud of them and their children. All four are college graduates and are successful in their lives and professional careers.

Renewal – Rebirth: New Responsibilities

1980 – 1991

Even if you're on the right track, you'll get run over if you just sit there.

-Will Rogers

What can you say about a society that says God is dead and Elvis is alive?

- Irv Kupcinet

At the end of the 1979-80 school year, I was very abruptly transferred from my principalship to district office work. My job was to evaluate the guidance department effectiveness in the four secondary schools and improve their image among students, teachers, administrators, and especially parents. My new title was principal of guidance (ouch). Although I felt let down by the unwanted transfer and embarrassed by the way it came down. (I was informed after the last day of school, so I couldn't say thanks and good-bye to the staff, students, and parents).

However, I knew from previous meetings the superintendent had with our four secondary principals regarding his concerns about the effectiveness of our district's guidance program and leadership, that at some time soon, a concerted effort to study the problems, find new directions, and new leadership was a high priority. I also knew through the grapevine that the superintendent wanted to improve the high school administrative staff. To promote one of the current high school assistant principals to be considered for the principalship at the high school, he saw the opportunity to kill two birds with one stone. By transferring me to do the guidance project, and making the high school assistant principal my replacement, he achieved his goal. So, knowing this plan, it helped me accept my new role, which turned out to be a growth experience, and needed change, although I couldn't foresee it at the time.

After a semester of observing the guidance counselors, doing a needs assessment of the students, parents, teachers and administrators, I was ready to start writing my evaluation report and recommendations for the superintendent. I also included extensive research from colleges, New York, and numerous other state education departments. It took several months to bring it all together. I thought it was thorough and well done.

I'll never forget, however, getting back the draft I sent the superintendent. It had more written corrections than my content. More than half was crossed out, and I was told how to redo it, what to include, and what format to use, including graphs and charts. It took me a while to bounce back from this criticism, but looking back, the final product (some fifty pages) was a better document.

The report and recommendations were made to the school board who accepted it and implemented all the changes I suggested. One of the first was to discontinue the practice of the secondary principals using guidance counselors for administrative purposes (scheduling, keeping records, making written reports of achievement, etc.) but to let them use their time to counsel students and parents. We developed a guidance curriculum for grades K-12 (proactive, planned lessons, activities, and outcomes for students and parents on career and college planning) and opened a career and college guidance office in the local public library, which was open to students and parents from 10:00 A.M. to 9:00 P.M. Monday through Saturday and 12:00-5:00 P.M. on Sunday. The computer-assisted college placement programs were available there also. It became very popular, to the point where parents from surrounding districts were using these readily available guidance services, which is what parents wanted.

In September of 1981, my district office duties were expanded. I became principal of student support services and was put in charge of special education and the Committee on Special Education. A new director of guidance was hired, and my work was turned over to him. I was out of the high school closet and now a real member of district office staff. My penance was hopefully, over. I stayed in district office for the next ten years, mostly serving in roles that included special education, supervising the school nurses, medical services, drug abuse prevention programs, health education, and obtaining grants, etc. I enjoyed these years. The scope of the work was much wider, challenging, and you had more autonomy and authority being in district office. The downside was the long hours, attending every school board meeting, and representing district office at all school functions. It was common to have one to two evening meetings a week. It went with the territory.

But there were rewarding moments. My most treasured experience and of which I'm proud was when I served on a N.Y. State Education Steering Committee developing the HIV/AIDS health education unit. That year, I was also serving as president of the New York State Pupil Support Services Administrators and in that capacity, was invited to serve on the steering committee.

We met in Albany for two days to make recommendations. Everyone was paranoid because it required new sex education, at an earlier age. I suggested each school system should establish its own ad hoc committee consisting of; a broad spectrum of community clergypersons, local physicians, P.T.A. reps, health education teacher, a parent of an elementary, middle, and high school student, and a district office administrator. This nucleus would debate and gather consensus to make curriculum recommendations made by the steering committee to the local board of education. My objective was to take the heat off the school board. They are the ultimate volunteers and deal with enough problems. This issue was complex and value sensitive. My recommendation became part of the new commissioner's regulations and mandatory for the whole state! Made me feel worthy. And it worked! Our local committee's recommendations were fully accepted by the school board and implemented K-12 in all of our schools.

Another highlight of my service in district office was our district's participation in a federally and state-funded comprehensive drug abuse prevention program. I had heard about the program (AUNTI-Adelphi University National Training Institute) sponsored by the U.S. Office of Education from colleagues in other districts. I wrote a grant for our district to participate, which was approved. It required the active involvement of the school board, superintendent, principals, teachers, parents, and a member of the local police department. We were trained at the Southampton Inn during long residential stays. During the 1981-83 school years, I stayed a total of twenty-six nights at the Southampton Inn as coordinator of the program.

Gerald Edwards, Ed. D., who was the best trainer, professor, and mentor I ever experienced, directed the AUNTI program. The school district still has many of the programs we started and some new ones. This training, and the follow-up activities, grants, and programs I developed were the most satisfying and rewarding work of my career. Dr. Edwards put much-needed wind and new directions into my sails (and several other administrators). I still use many of his lessons and communication techniques in the classes I taught at Dowling College. His teaching methods work, and I'm eternally grateful to him.

The AUNTI program had a refreshing take on and philosophy of prevention. Gerry's definition was that prevention activities are proactive experiences that are intentionally designed to help people manage potentially difficult life situations, (rather than focus on end-state conditions – drug use or addiction). The purpose of prevention was to understand the antecedent behaviors and attitudes that could lead to drug abuse, alienation, poor communication, and self-assertive skills, inadequate self-concept or support system, lack of goals, shallow character, etc. Also, the bombardment of constant commercials and billboards, as well as newspaper and magazine stories about promoting alcohol, tobacco, and other drugs. Actually, tobacco and alcohol are the real "gateway" drugs, not just pot.

The program was designed to help students, parents, and educators to see the big picture and understand the complexity of the problem. Starting in the elementary schools, students need to learn effective communication skills, including resistance, self-assertive skills, to be able to say no, and feel comfortable with that decision. As the grades progress, more accurate information on the deleterious effects of drugs on self and family should be presented. Further, it's important to establish proactive support activities like MADD (Mothers Against Drunk Driving), peer leadership groups in all schools to generate meaningful, wholesome activities to keep kids happy and high on life, and their lives.

To prevent alienation, one of the programs I started in our elementary schools was the Primary Mental Health Project started by a psychologist at the University of Rochester, geared for grades kindergarten through third grade. We ran our program with parent volunteers (after training) to spend separate "special" time with students that teachers identified as loners, isolated, or lacking friends. I even volunteered and enjoyed my time with my new little friends!

The training we received from Dr. Edwards and his staff was all participative, interactive, self- and group-growth activities. These included; group dynamics, leadership skills, communication skills, and learning to apply the Synectic Problem Solving Model to help generate meaningful new drug abuse prevention strategies and programs. The breadth and depth of these experiential activities created a new awareness of our outer and inner worlds through the growth process of serious introspection. You were able to see yourself and society more objectively, with greater understanding.

I felt I was back in graduate school again, but on dedicated time we had together made the efforts more worthwhile and productive. The effect of the training was deeply felt. I know I applied it throughout the rest of my career. Some of the high school teachers perceived their colleagues that went to the AUNTI training programs being so different they referred to them as "Born Again" teachers. Nice complement.

I also enjoyed working with and learning from the superintendent of schools, Henry R. He was an excellent administrator and had the ability to cut to the chase of issues, see the big picture, and always planned one or two years ahead. He worked very well with the board of education. We became friends as well as colleagues.

Throughout my thirty-two years in public education as a teacher, principal, and district level (K-12) administrator, I was amazed at the amount of change that took place. Change was the only constant. The curriculum changed frequently, driven by national or state mandates, professional persuasion (trends), textbook, or software companies. National, state, and standardized tests were changed in content and format. Requirements for graduation and teacher certification were raised. Parental involvement switched from being supportive to somewhat combative. Standards for students, including dress codes, lessened each year. There was lack of support and you constantly had to adapt and accept the situation de jour. You learned to tolerate change and expect it. The present meant more than past traditions and expectations. Positive role models were sorely lacking, especially entertainers, celebrities, religious leaders, professional athletes, and politicians, that youth could look up to and emulate.

Perhaps the most difficult changes to accept for many in the 80's and 90's was the HIV/AIDS epidemic and the "coming out" of the gay subculture. Male gays, especially if they had effeminate behaviors, were mocked. Lesbians as individuals were not obvious, but when they were with their partner, were more apparent. Yet there was more tolerance for female gays. HIV/AIDS required school systems to hold workshops on the at-risk-causative factors as well as provide an HIV/AIDS protection kit. There was real fear of getting HIV/AIDS from a student. It took time for the anxiety to lessen. The problem(s) is not outside, but inside ourselves.

Minorities (Black, Hispanic) had developed political and rights-advocate groups. You had to really think through any disciplinary action you would take, especially with minority students, to be sure of your facts, and that you were being fair and impartial. If you didn't do your homework, you might have a hard time defending against the "extended family" (NAACP, etc.) that often would come to the defense of the student and their family.

You had to anticipate public relations problems that could escalate a minor, normal behavioral incident into a nightmare of public overreaction. I never had a problem with this new sensitivity and cultural consciousness since I felt disadvantaged myself and knew what it was like to be an underdog. The minority groups simply and rightly wanted the playing field to be level. They did not want to be treated differently, just the same as whites. That was the dilemma then, and now.

Even teachers (especially male) started to "dress down." Everything seemed to be getting loose. The normal customs and manners of the past were obsolete. I was living, and working, in a different, but not better world.

My salary in my final year (1990-1991) was $85,000. Now, on Long Island, many teachers at the top of the salary schedule, with sixty credits of graduate study beyond the master's, earn over $100,000. I'm so pleased to see the significance of our labors finally being recognized. Teachers deserve every penny earned and then some. It's very difficult, important, and demanding work. It creates our future.

However, reflecting on our current decline in achievement and progress in educational reforms, significant changes have to manifest in the delivery systems of effective instruction (teaching – learning process) especially in reading, math, and science, increasing the length of the school day and year, expanding pre–K education. Funding mechanisms need to be proactive, top priority, and progressive (not relying on regressive real estate taxes).

Perhaps the most important practical and immediate change needed in the future for public education is to develop a fair, yet significant increase in funding mechanisms. At present, most states rely on a regressive real estate tax and proceeds that are supposed to go to education from lottery programs (most of which are diverted to the general fund). The problem gets worse every year, especially with the understandable backlash from high taxes from the ever-increasing population of retired senior citizens. New York State, to cite an example I'm most familiar with, has convened several "blue ribbon" panels to come up with better ways of adequately funding public education only to find their recommendations rejected by politicians. So school systems have to fight the battle of a budget vote each year and face the reality of going on an austerity budget. This is a ludicrous, obscene, and self-defeating process.

Unless American culture and society agrees that children *are important* and *truly valued,* we will stumble along with inadequate misplaced priorities. We mouth a good game when it comes to children and recognize them at holidays. But if we look at the realities and statistics of child abuse, abortion, child and teenage suicide, teenage pregnancy, alcohol, tobacco and drug abuse, drop out and low graduations rates, runaways, etc., we begin to see a society that doesn't really care.

School funding will improve when we place the success of the future generations as our *number-one priority* and demand our government take care of our domestic problems rather than the smoke and mirror games of getting involved in other countries that don't want our presence. I pray I live to see the day money gets diverted from the pentagon, to help P.T.A's support school efforts by not having them raise monies through cakes sales, raffles, and car washes. America must walk it's talk, and put the money where the truly important values are, ...like *effective public education for all children.*

Parents also need support through the developmental stages and changes their children, and they, go through. Schools should develop and implement parenting skills education programs to help parents proactively meet the changes and problems (which are normal) as they go thru nursery, elementary, middle, high school, and college. Ideal, yes, and needed, certainly. American society tends to be end-state condition oriented, letting problems manifest into crisis, rather than take proactive positive action at the sources (causes) of problems that prevent them.

A major problem for our children (and ourselves) is the phenomenon of age compression. Children are bombarded by TV programs, commercials, cyberspace, etc. that promote sexuality, use of alcohol, tobacco, other drugs, and violence. Parents have to be vigilant to prevent the glorification of ego fulfillment, and self-destructive behaviors as portrayed by the media as norms. Young children are dressing, using makeup, and acting like miniature adults long before they should.

Children need age appropriate models and messages. They need to develop normally in a wholesome maturational process, gaining solid, safe and sound values. Our society compresses adult behaviors into children who are not ready or should be open to such inputs.

Many adults are also caught up in this psychosocial aberrance. Instead of leaving adolescence, they remain arrested as a fifteen-year-old throughout their adulthood. So, in addition to age compression effects on children, we also see results of late, if any, maturity expansion in many adults, life-long adolescence, rather than becoming a mature adult.

Television, high-tech devices, cyberspace amusements, etc., tend to capture children's and adolescent's attention. When deprived of these immediate gratification sources, they become easily bored and restless. Parents tend to further facilitate external involvement through organized activities like; athletic teams, dancing classes, martial arts, etc., which creates an overloaded time schedule skewed by the children's (needs), placing stress on the entire family.

This promotion of "play" requires little, if any, planning and creativity on the part of the "involved" child. This child-oriented culture has created children who need to be entertained; fun and more fun is their mantra. This promotes the condition of ennui, a feeling of annoyance, weariness, dissatisfaction, and boredom with life. Ennui is seen in classrooms where children resent the needed drills, application, and practice required for successful achievement of subject matter. Teachers have to increase their use of visual teaching-learning methods to keep the students in the classroom engaged in the active, participative process of learning. Self-discipline and responsibility are waning from our society.

All Americans need to develop and implement a common mission statement and business plan that will fulfill the Constitution. Let's begin with charity at home, each home, community, county, and state. We desperately need inspired, passionate, purposeful, leaders who steer the course needed by a strong moral compass. To paraphrase Victor Hugo. Will is everything. Problem is... we're wanting in will and courage to do the right thing, rather than the "popular" or "politically correct" thing.

Looking back on my career, I'm proud I became an educator. For it was my teachers that took me from being Clifford Bennett, Jr. that I hated, to accept Buddy Bennett until I was mature and secure enough to be Cliff. Thanks to them, I can now be Clifford; it's okay to be me.

I hope I've helped others in their journey with the transitions they had to make. Teaching is the noblest of professions. Teaching is the one profession that makes all the others possible. It is a meaningful, satisfying, challenging choice.

Transition to Higher Education

Back to College
1991 – 2001

Teaching at Dowling College

The hardest arithmetic to master is that which enables us to count our blessings.

- Eric Hoffer

Opportunities are usually disguised by hard work, so most people don't recognize them.

- Ann Landers

I retired in August 1991 after thirty-two years in the profession—seven teaching, fourteen as principal, and eleven as a district office administrator. The N.Y.S. teachers retirement system was offering a .06 percent incentive, and I decided to take it, which, gave me a pension of 70 percent of my final average salary. The pension requirements for teachers now are much different. They have to work longer and get fewer benefits. Change is the only constant.

At the time fifty-five seems like a good age to retire. Looking back, it's much too young. You are really at your peak then, and continue to be productive; the decision to retire is a difficult one. Retire from something, yes, but to what?

So right after I retired, like so many others, I thought I would become a consultant. I had a business card made up (Challenging Choices) and became a public business. Little did I know how many other retirees and wanabees are also consultants! Without a network or leads, all you do is put your card in the bowl with the others and hope.

Think twice about the realities of consulting. It's very hard to get your foot in the door, much less walk through it. I suggest that if you don't have viable things to do to give your life meaning and purpose, don't retire. The concept of retirement is an old paradigm from the industrial revolution for those few that got their gold watch. Be sure retirement is too something, not just from routine. You'll soon miss it and be bored out of your gourd. Your job is a gift. You may not miss the work, but you'll miss the people.

The transition to retirement was very difficult for me. The day you retire is like instant invisibility. You have no office, no secretary, no colleagues, no support system, and no formal purpose. Given our life expectancy is now longer than before, that's almost twenty years (hopefully more) of retirement. Fortunately for me, I had been teaching in-service courses for the local BOCES, and had taught part time at Hofstra University from 1961-1968.

I also had twenty-seven articles published in numerous professional journals during my career, so I felt confident I could get work teaching at a local college.

I was fortunate to be able to be hired by Dowling College, Oakdale, New York, ten miles from my home, as an adjunct assistant professor of education and field supervisor of student teachers. Between the two roles, I worked as much as I wanted to, and felt productive; I didn't think I could go "cold turkey" into retirement at the age fifty-five. I now value my remaining years and want to travel, fish, play golf, and enjoy my wife, children, and especially grandchildren. It's time to smell the roses before I'm not around to sniff. This was brought home when I learned of my sister Gloria's death in November, 1991. She died of a heart attack at the age of seventy-four. She was supportive and helpful to me. I miss her.

Although I had some experience in higher education (teaching as an adjunct instructor at Hofstra College 1961-1968) I really became immersed when I worked at Dowling College (1991-2001) as both an adjunct assistant professor of education and clinical supervisor of student teachers. I enjoyed every minute of it, especially coaching the student teachers. My favorite was teaching graduate courses, primarily human relations for teachers, and methods of teaching science. I had much autonomy and loved that. It was great to be back in the classroom. The secretarial staff was most helpful and friendly. They made it a pleasant work environment.

I am proud to be associated with Dowling for ten years. I've witnessed it grow into a fine college, with cutting edge contemporary programs, especially in undergraduate and graduate education programs. Dowling now has two campuses. I taught at both. I love the Oakdale campus on the Connetquot River. It's a beautiful setting, ideal for their crew teams, and conferences.

Higher education is very different from public school education and in some ways, similar. In higher education you are more autonomous and independent. No one is looking over your shoulder, and there is little supervision or evaluation. There are differences in the political dynamics. In the public schools the community and parents play politics, and the superintendent and school board play their own kind. You have to be on your toes not to displease the wrong people and, at the same time, ingratiate yourself to the power players, even to the extent of joining the "correct" service club. The politics are more external.

At the university level, the politics are mostly internal and hierarchical. The organizational structure and layers are thick and many; titles, degrees, tenure, and longevity, all play much more important roles than the dynamics of people. Starting with the all-powerful president, thru the provost, deans of schools, department heads, and professors' union. Adjuncts could not teach more than eighteen hours, which is the equivalent of six courses in an academic year. The irony to that was, part-time faculty taught more courses than full-time. You knew your place and as long as you didn't make waves and received favorable evaluations from the students, you were okay.

However, there was always pressure on the full-time faculty to "publish or perish," do significant research, or give workshops and lectures to get the college name known. Professors had formal evaluations annually, usually by their peers. There was usually stress and one-up-manship going on between them.

I remember co-authoring the student teacher handbook and finding out our names could not appear, but our initials could be used. We were told by the dean it was because we were adjuncts and not full time. After my co-author and I retired, we noticed our initials were gone and new names (completely spelled out) appeared in the handbook as the authors. It's a different world. Tender relationships between full and part timers. Status and layers of perceived professionalism is important in the world of higher education. Be careful what you say. Play the game. Be a survivor. Never say no.

To this day, I do not understand the escalating costs, seemingly every year, of college tuition. The fees for one and one-half graduate students' tuition paid my teaching stipend at Dowling College. Adjuncts usually receive no fringe benefits. Considering I averaged twenty-three to twenty-five students in my classes, I would think the other costs are more than met. What's obscene today in major universities (especially division one) is the amount of budget that goes toward athletics, especially coaches' salaries. We should be rewarding cutting-edge research, excellence in teaching undergraduate and graduate students, not playing public relations through athletic recognition. Only in America!

The teaching-learning process in "higher" education needs vast improvement. Content (knowledge) is king. Process (learning – effective teaching methods) is less important. The predominate method of teaching in college is still lecturing (current research shows that 70 percent of professors still consider the lecture format their primary mode of instruction). To add insult to injury, some professors have the audacity to lecture while sitting, or leaning on a podium. There is little, if any, feedback from students to teacher. Classes are so large, they're held in auditoriums or "lecture halls" where you never get to interact with the professor (who doesn't know your name anyway.)

College administration, along with faculty unions, need to implement in-service ongoing, training for all levels of faculty, in research-based effective methods of teaching,... especially multi-modality learning (use of varied teaching methods that involve all senses). In addition to a department of education, there has to be concern for effective education in each department. Achieving terminal degrees and publishing scholarly articles and books is impressive in that it demonstrates <u>excellent learning</u>. However, of equal importance is the <u>ability to teach</u>,... to impart love for learning, enjoying students personally, challenging growth, and making learning interesting and understandable for all students.

I find it fascinating that the only place you can fail is in a school. The blame and shame comes down on the students. Could it be the teacher or system has "failed"? Why do we blame the student, rather then all the responsible parties involved? Could it be the gas was no good rather than a defective engine? I propose we do away with the concept of failure and replace it with the average numerical "grade" earned. Given the criteria for competence: ninety to one hundred, outstanding, eighty to ninety, excellent, etc. below sixty-five, unacceptable - does not meet minimum competency standards. If the student gets a fifty-eight average, it speaks for itself that they did not yet demonstrate minimum competence. He or she didn't "fail." It was an unsuccessful attempt (unacceptable), and we now go on for remediation until we master the skills (knowledge, attitude, and proficiency) to show minimum competence. Students need to "buy" into *their* responsibility for learning and for meeting the obligations and requirements for demonstrating competence. All parts of the educational system dynamics (teacher, student, parent(s), adaptive – assistive technology, etc.) need to share the *responsibility* for <u>getting the student to acceptable performance</u>.

Not all students will be scholars or on the honor roll. There should be a community two-year college for every student (able and wanting to do the work), but four years of college should not be an expectation for every student. Some kids want other things for their lives and go on to be successful, contributing members of society. What I'm suggesting is to take the sting and stigma out of poor performance by calling it failure. Isn't it paradoxical that the only place I can think of the concept of failure being applied is a school? The feedback a student (or any person) needs is he or she didn't achieve the minimum standard and what is needed to improve.

Global labels like you failed discourage learning. Imagine if Edison had quit after each unsuccessful attempt. Educators should be more supportive, caring, and optimistic about a student's future and less punitive minded. Children need to learn about natural consequences and self-responsibility, perseverance, and how to improve their knowledge, skills, proficiency, and attitude. <u>Diagnosis, prescription and remediation is needed, not a grade of F.</u>

Educators need to look at *their* responsibilities to promote effective, *achieved* learning. Lets stop making the student(s) and/or parent(s) "failures." We need to focus on the main cognitive functions of thinking, learning, feeling, and remembering. These need to be met with challenges, help, outreach, inspiration, and love,... not Fs. Who co-owns the problem and can help the most? We all can, with the student.

Our current educational system functions as a zero-sum sport (win/lose). All players have the potential to be successful, albeit with lower "scores" than others. What matters is doing your best, and, if needed, remediation to help stay the course. Our mind set, when win/win, would prevent discouragement, especially perceptions of inadequacy, weakness and blame from "failing". All students need encouragement to foster confidence, faith, hope and optimism about themselves, and their future. <u>Learning is work in constant progress.</u> Both teacher and student need to apply more patience, practice and perseverance to achieve mastery of content as well as skill proficiency.

Interim Administrative Positions

Happy Days – New Homes
New Challenges
1993-2001

Nowadays we think of a philanthropist as someone who donates big sums of money, yet the word is derived from two Greek words, philos **(loving) and** anthropos **(man): loving man. All of us are capable of being philanthropists. We can give of ourselves.**

- Edward Lindsey

The best and most beautiful things in the world cannot be seen or even touched—they must be felt with the heart.

- Helen Keller

———————————•———————————

To date, the highlight of the consulting work I have done in retirement, has been my interim administrative positions in special education in the Center Moriches and East Quogue School Districts, and especially my six-month stint as the principal of the Eagle Elementary School in the Patchogue-Medford School District (Jan.-June 1998). I found the working environments, parents, colleagues, and administrators further out east on Long Island to be more relaxed and friendly. It's almost a time warp. In East Quogue, the respect, courtesy, and cooperation was wonderful. It is a beautiful school and community.

Having worked in secondary schools almost my entire career, my six months as an elementary school principal were refreshing. The teachers at Eagle Elementary were very professional and child oriented. The students respected and even hugged you! The principal was a father figure substitute (in my case, grandfather). In a secondary school, you're viewed more as if you were from the CIA, ATF, and FBI, by faculty and students.

Two experiences at Eagle stand out as signs of changing times. I received a phone call from the director of the after-school care program at another Elementary School, that one of my second graders had threatened to bring in a gun the next day to shoot this other boy. Since there was so much violence going on in schools throughout the country, especially with handguns, I felt I had to be thorough and follow up on this situation.

So the next morning, I told the student's teacher to bring him to me as soon as he arrived on the bus platform, complete with his winter coat, backpack, and lunch box. With the teacher as a witness, I searched his coat, backpack, and lunch box for a weapon. He had none. I asked him if he had threatened this other boy at the Canaan Elementary School, where the after school program was held. He said he did. When I asked if there was a handgun at home, he said there was. His mom was a single parent of three boys, all attended Eagle.

I immediately called his mother, told her why I wanted to have a conference, and that I was also calling the police. I told both to arrive in about an hour. I asked the mother to come in to explain the seriousness of his threat in light of what was happening at schools like Columbine. She agreed. I asked the police officer to just write up a report of the incident and to underscore my concern for the mother to be vigilant in watching her son. The police officer was magnificent!

Imagine a cop in uniform, sitting on my desk talking very seriously, but age appropriately, about the reality of what the student had said to the other boy. At one point, he opened his shirt to show his bulletproof vest and asked the boy if he knew why he was wearing it. He said he didn't know. So the police officer explained that guns shoot bullets that kill people, and the vest was to prevent the bullet from injuring him. He also told him that if he had brought a gun to school, and if he was called, that if he pointed the gun at him, thinking he might shoot him, he might have to shoot the boy. He asked him if he knew what this meant. He vaguely understood. But the message was delivered loud and clear to child and parent.

The police officer left after giving me the report. I explained the severity of the situation to the mother and suspended the boy from school for three days. I wrote a dramatic letter to the mother and copied the police report as an attachment to the letter to drive home the concern for this behavior and to prevent it in the future. I also wrote a very positive letter of thanks to the police officer for being such a good educator, copying the commissioner and precinct commander. Welcome to the schools of the 1990's! And this was in an elementary school!

The other incident was also an eye-opener, especially as to how parents have changed over my forty years in dealing with them. Part of my daily routine while I was at Eagle, was to check the behavior of the students in the cafeteria during lunch periods. Much to my chagrin, the students were often too loud, touched or punched each other, and got up from their tables (often running) without permission. I couldn't believe that the teachers did not have to supervise the cafeteria. The union negotiated that out of the contract. Only the lunchroom monitors supervised, and they had no authority in the eyes of the students. The cafeteria behavior (and on the buses) was the worst part of the elementary school experience.

During one lunch period, I was correcting student's misbehavior as I walked amongst the tables. The tattling was unbelievable. I grabbed one fourth-grade boy by the shoulder as he ran by, failing to listen to me, and stop. I took him back to the table and wrote the incident in the classroom teacher's lunch behavior book, which the monitors did, with the intent the classroom teacher would correct or discipline the student (in class). This process didn't work well. I forgot the incident, since it was so common.

As soon as I entered the school office the next morning, the secretary informed me a fourth-grade boy's irate father was waiting to see me. I told her to give me a minute to hang up my coat, and send him in. He came into my office with his two boys; one was in kindergarten. He was obviously upset and very angry that some male staff member had "assaulted" his son yesterday, and showed me a slight black and blue mark on his upper left shoulder. I still wasn't making the association with what happened yesterday in the cafeteria. I didn't think the father was talking about me, until he added insult to injury, by asking his kindergarten son to tell me how much I hurt his brother. (The kindergarten boy was not present when this happened, but was being used as an eyewitness.) He was talking about me! I couldn't believe it. At least now I knew who the "culprit" was!

I explained the chronic behavior problems in the cafeteria to the father and that I did grab his son by the shoulder because he was running, could have fallen, or hurt another child, and didn't stop when I told him to. He told me he didn't know if he was going to report me to Child Protective Services, call the police, or call the superintendent. I reminded him he was talking to the principal, that I was doing my job, that his son was breaking school rules, and I did not mean to hurt his boy. I also told him he could do whatever he wanted. I was running out of patience and being put on trial by this father and his two children was a bit much. I apologized to the boy and father, but told them I was only doing my job. The father left, and I never heard from him again. From that moment on, I swore I would never touch another child unless it was an emergency.

Again, welcome to American schools in the 1990's. Some parents sure have changed. And we wonder why the schools have discipline problems? Who has co-ownership of the problem? Are parents preventing teachers and administrators from showing affection, concern, or love? Is appropriate, needed touching off limits? I hope not.

Achieving Balance and Growth in a Changing World

1980 - 2001

We are continuously faced with a series of great opportunities brilliantly disguised as insoluble problems.

- John W. Gardner

Some people think it's holding on that makes one strong, sometimes it's letting go.

- Sylvia Robinson

———————●———————

Because our country is so young, we do not have much history or a dominant culture or religion that instilled values that reflected a core belief system. Our society basically inherited its major cultural influence from English history. We accepted democracy and many aspects of British law and legal systems as our own. While these supply stability for process, our society is so complex, with so many nationalities and religions, that it creates great diversity. Change is rapid and constant. Our "culture" is a work in progress.

Values in our society change very rapidly because of the variety of subcultures that make up our "culture". Liberal politicians and judges, youth emphasis, skin-deep beauty, gays, media, movies, TV, generational emphasis (teenagers, preteens), sports, celebrities, advertising, and the latest technology in communication and games, all promote the focus on *me*, immediate gratification, and create people who are conditioned into multitasking.

In a sense, America does not have a culture. It's both our strength and our weakness that flux is the norm. It's difficult to be a parent (and especially a grandparent) because of the values, imprints, and conditioning experiences that creates the "norms" of living for each generation. These "gaps" can cause communication and expectation differences that promote artificial chasms between the generations. A significant example of change in attitudes seen in our value system now, is my generations' emphasis on living your life to: assume <u>responsibilities</u> and <u>obligations</u>, whereas today's generation, is to affirm their "rights" and "freedoms". These differences are just reflections of the social-cultural ingrained influences that were absorbed during our formative years. We need to bridge and understand these "gaps", as normal outcomes of differing values.

In my worldview, I'm proud I was a teacher, administrator, and college professor. It's certainly not my wealth status that brings me contentment, but the knowledge that I did make a difference and tried to make teaching and learning enjoyable. Looking back on my forty-two years as an educator, I could see mega differences and changes in the profession, however.

I found some teachers were insecure and did *not* tolerate change well. They wanted the security of their classroom and feeling they needed to be in control. The principal or parent(s) were supposed to have "magic dust" to sprinkle on children that did not obey or were troubled students. They did not understand that a society gets the crime rate that it deserves and that the school they worked in, as their classroom, reflected the society and subcultures of the community. The classroom was supposed to be a constant, a castle of the past that wouldn't change and would remain sacrosanct from the real world.

Teacher unions have become stronger. They provide powerful negotiations and influence on the school board. My concern or issue with them is their contract underscores only *minimum* performance standards, rather than *maximum* or quality-total expectations. When I started teaching in '59, I was paid $200.00 as the stipend to coach freshmen football. Now the coaches' salaries are a percentage of the teachers' salary schedule in the thousands of dollars. Teachers have negotiated away many supervisory responsibilities (they call them extra duties) like lunchroom supervision. If they "volunteer" for these duties, they get paid an *extra* wage (usually the hourly rate for home teaching). Administrators are obligated to follow the contract to the letter, or face grievance procedures that are time consuming and teacher oriented. So, the teachers end up with a powerful extensive support system, while the school administrators have no "union" and really no support system at all.

There is a necessity for teachers' unions. They protect and improve working conditions, provide fellowship and support. However, a balance of influence, leadership and responsibility has to be shared with other major stakeholders in public education to increase collective vision of what is, and isn't, working to achieve common educational goals. For example, school district newsletters that report high school graduation information, should focus on all students in that class, including those that "dropped out", transferred out, and a complete breakdown by percentages of those that actually graduated and went on to: four year colleges, community college, trade-technical schools, military service, work, etc. In addition, a longitudinal study should be made of each graduating class every year, for the next four consecutive years, reporting percentages of how many actually: graduated from college, transferred to another institution, are employed, or can't find a job, etc. This information would help monitor the effectiveness of the K-12 education of all students and give all major stakeholders: school administrators, teachers, parents, school boards, etc., input for analysis and improvement.

As one of my graduate school professors opined, "Be kind to all of your students, no matter how bad their behavior is, or poor academic success. You may run into them as the president of the board of education or chief of the local fire department when you need them in the future." How true. How wise.

Now it's time to look ahead and continue to grow and learn. To ask better, wiser questions. To accept some have no answer, except yours. I have many more teachers to meet and lessons to be learned. When your mind is ready, a teacher will appear. What a wonderful adventure life is! I will survive as long as I keep finding balance and hope. Accept and be open to invitations to grow from life, by making challenging choices.

I'm glad to see many school districts including character education in the curriculum K-12. It is desperately needed to help our young people understand they live in an interdependent world. We all need to practice the character expressed by Thomas Aquinas, "We are all born angels, except with only one wing. We learn to fly by embracing each other."

Perhaps the most important course in embracing (which I'm still taking) is my experiences becoming the only caregiver for my sister, Phoebe, who is now eighty-seven. When her husband, Walter, passed away in 1998, she was in the hospital (for the forty-fifth time in her life) recovering from surgery for diverticulitis and a colostomy. I had to help get her through these phase transformations (inner and outer changes), which was difficult since Phoebe's health and coping skills were poor. Her usual reply to your prompting her to do something you think she could do is, ... "I can't."

Phoebe wanted to go to a nursing home, despite my encouragement to try living at home or in an assisted living facility. She requested to go to the Lutheran Home for the Aging in Smithtown, where she still is. For Phoebe to become eligible for Medicaid, she (I) had to "spend down" her assets to $3,000.00. Much to my surprise, I found that Phoebe and Walter had $400,000 in CDs and savings accounts in four different banks. All of this went to the nursing home, so she would be accepted by Medicaid.

How it hurt to see this money disappear, that Phoebe and Walter never enjoyed a penny from their life savings. It made me realize how important it is to live life while you can and that we really don't need more money than for our necessities. More importantly, to have good health, a strong sense of humor, optimistic outlook toward life, and be creative, are the only free essentials we need to transit during our rental time here in earth school.

Going to the nursing home is not a pleasant outing. Between the smell of urine and constant cries of "Help me, take me home, I want my mother," etc., it is depressing. Couple that with Phoebe's demands for things she could ask for, or do for herself, it is not a fun visit. After a while, you get tired of her learned helplessness, especially,..... "I can't."

However, you must transcend how you are feeling and realize your obligation is to provide support and love even though you feel it is not being appreciated, or wonder why you've been given the role of caregiver? It's difficult to go beyond ourselves, but it's God's way of putting us in our place, by giving us perspective on why we should be grateful, and to transcend to a higher level of selfless love.

Surviving and Thriving

Turning Points
2001 – Present

Is it progress if a cannibal uses a knife and fork?

- Stanilow J. Lee

*Character, in the long run, is the decisive factor
in the life of an individual and nations alike.*

- Theodore Roosevelt

There is more to life than increasing its speed.

- Mohandas K. Gandhi

*A cynic is a man who, when he smells flowers, looks
around for a coffin.*

- H. L. Mencken

*At all costs we must re-establish faith in spiritual values.
We must worship something beyond ourselves,
lest we destroy ourselves.*

- Phillip Gibbs

———————•———————

To get the most from this final chapter, I've included five of my poems, to help you understand the changes in my personal and worldview as I've lived through the first decade of the twenty-first century. These will add perspective on what follows now.

My purpose in these next few pages is to help you *accept differences* in life, rather than magnify them. Understand that my take on these changes has been filtered through a senior citizens memory bank, and are shaped by old imprints and conditioning that are different from what I've been accustomed. I, too, need to change.

AUTHENTIC

Where went
And where can
We find
Things genuine
And not advertised?

HIGH TECH – POTENTIAL WRECK

Getting tired, feeling wired?
Does life seem undesired,
Need more than twenty-four hours,
To smell the flowers?

Multi-tasking may get you through
But the process will wear you out
Adjust your priorities, less is more
More is less, without doubt.

i-Phones, palm pilots, lap tops, cyberspace
Speed things up, create a new pace
Only to do more of the same
Not exactly a claim to fame.

Emerging, latest high-tech
Makes me a wreck.
I like simple tools that last
Old habits keep me in the past.

"LET'S ROLL!"

Where can we find
Pride deep inside
A code of humane conduct
Behavior we can respect

Character used to be
Virtue, dignity, morality
Now, it just reflects
Someone who disrespects authority

Flamboyantly different
Above all, arrogant
Going against the grain
Perhaps without a brain?

First it was Madonna
Now, we've got LADY GAGA
Where did they get this shameless fame?
We all have to share that blame

With no more delay
Let's stop character decay
Be a believer
Remember Todd Beamer!

Get With it!

This world is changing so fast
I seem to have no relevant past
Change is so constant and steady
I don't know how to be ready.

Up seems down, down is up
I'm caught on a speed bump
My own worst enemy,
Not being in the twenty-first century.

Living through the beginning of the twenty-first century has been quite a wake-up call. I feel I'm living in a different, confusing, strange, busy world than the one I grew up in. I'm aware that change is the only constant in life. Yet, our improved means (speed, variety, media messages) seem to create impoverished ends. I'm not sure the current and emerging state of affairs is improving the quality of life. We seem to need to multitask, just to get through a normal day.

Life in America has become more complicated, less simple. An example is the numerous choices we now have to go through before buying cereal. Choices were limited to Puffed Rice, Corn Flakes, Wheaties, or Shredded Wheat; now there are cereals of countless variety. The same is true of almost every item you buy. We accept consumerism as normal, become spoiled, and expect the latest trends and "coolest" gadgets.

Compounding the plethora of products available to us, is the twenty-four/seven continuous bombardment of clever, enticing TV and other advertising media. We are led to believe we're diminished or not complete, yet we're better off than most countries in the world. I often think while the TV remote has been a helpful innovation; we are not in control of the content, just the process of selecting channels. In a sense, it has made us believe we're in control and that life can be programmed and changed while sitting or lying down. This device, while a marvelous convenience, has added to our apathetic and lazy attitude to do less.

Another type of dissociation from former reality is caused by our senses becoming numbed and, blurred, by the rapid fire, creative images of advertisements. We look at one page, and see pictures of the unfolding horror of the Gulf of Mexico made oil "spill." Adjacent to this page is an ad for Lexus cars or a beautiful young model showing off the latest bra from Victoria's Secret.

These constant contrasting juxtapositions of "reality" affect your ability to determine what's real. Your feelings and emotions go for a roller-coaster ride, from feeling sorry or empathic, to disbelief or indifference. The differing pictures (or stories) challenge your perception of what's really going on in the world, at least the one conveyed to us by the media.

Also, our society tolerates erosion of standards and ethical behavior. Can we be objective about our current state of affairs seen in just living in America? We need to see our social problems of; poverty, homelessness, national debt, energy reliance, job opportunities, immigration, crime, percentage of U.S. citizens incarcerated, teenage and unwed pregnancies, tobacco, alcohol and drug addiction, highway carnage, unequal health care, support for public education, etc., as critical. These should become our highest immediate priorities for proactive, comprehensive, effective solutions. Yet, we seem to limp along, accepting these as normal. We need to heed the admonishment in Proverbs 29:18,...**Where there is no vision, the people perish.**

In our local communities, we experience daily driving problems, albeit drunken drivers, drivers using cell phones or worse; texting. In supermarkets, stores, and waiting rooms we see a lack of civility, especially in manners or basic courtesy. Many parents do not properly supervise or correct their children's inappropriate public behavior and treat them like miniadults or worse, their equals (age compression).

Who owns this problem? We all do. Our collective level of conscious awareness of these erosions of civilized behavior has to increase, creating a critical mass effort to improve it. We are becoming (are?) a society/culture that overvalues materialism, and promotes narcissism, and immediate gratification. This national concern and awareness is critical.

Unfortunately, a society gets the crime rate it deserves. We can, and need, to right the ship.

Polarizing our country, through the images created by media political superstars who are the spokespersons for ultraconservatives or liberal positions are splitting our nation into oppositional positions, a widening dichotomy. These political icons reflect narrow and extreme beliefs. Yet they have growing followers who would rather accept their radical viewpoints than objectively evaluate the complexity of today's world. We do not live in two dimensions, left or right.

Further confusing the public is how Congress feeds on how much press or airtime they get from various media, and in a reciprocal relationship, the media gets its motivation and information from the politicians to stay in business. It's a vicious cycle. This game being played is a win-win for the politicians, and media, but lose-lose for us.

We do not need gamesmanship. What we deserve and must get is <u>statesmanship</u> in government. Then, priorities on doing what's right for the greater good, rather then on one's own party or personal ambitions. The media need higher standards for balanced, objective reporting, and need to make our collective welfare their mission, not their bottom line. And wouldn't it be wonderful to have the media report regularly on <u>*all the good things*</u> that people do each day, rather than just reflecting bad news?

I hope that together, Congress, the executive office, and the media can right the ship. <u>We, the people, need:</u>

To regain trust, truth, and faith in our system of open government.

To practice common mutual priorities for two-way communication, collaboration, compromise, and synergy.

To stay connected to our forefathers' ideals and the constitution.

To develop stronger character, to live and lead purposeful, principled lives.

To daily practice the Golden Rule.

To climb together, to see brighter horizons, to value, learn from, and utilize our past, present, and future to create a better world.

Our political parties, especially their leaders and spokespersons, both left and right, need to walk their talk in the middle of the road, so we make real progress. We walk with both feet, for balance.

Our future is bright if we apply our will and determination to achieve these goals. We should not expect some miracle to achieve this. Everyone needs to take an active proactive role as responsible citizens. Let us apply the inspiration that we are given by Phillip Brooks:...

Do not pray for an easy life. Pray to be a stronger person. Do not pray for tasks equal to your powers. Pray for powers equal to your tasks. Then the doing of your work shall be no miracle, but you shall be the miracle.

To achieve our prayers, we need to be aware of the pressures put on us living in a Hedonistic culture. It is difficult to discipline oneself to resist groupthink and to independently, make different, difficult decisions to maintain control of our goals. We have to become stronger persons and keep our egos in check. Inner determination and strength are necessary to understand and holistically adapt to our rapidly changing external world. We have to accept differences in society from our own earlier experiences. To minimize evaluating the external world, especially social-cultural changes, to prevent becoming negative-chronic complainers, to embrace the here and now, and, go with the flow. We should heed the advice of Winston Churchill: "If we open a quarrel between the past and the present, we shall find that we have lost the future." To accept differences as what they are, just diverse, not right or wrong, will help us to grow in tolerance and to increase our vision. To prevent pessimism, we need to maintain a keen sense of humor, remain flexible, adaptive, and optimistic about the future.

Part of our adventure is being able to accept a changing world that seems to transform daily. It is difficult to understand and find meaning. We have to put continuous effort and energy into active listening and increasing our vision to coalesce and synthesize reality. This means we must learn to accept and understand change and, not fight, or ignore it.

We must remain flexible and principled—open, not closed. Hopeful. Willful. Connected.

We will survive and thrive by remembering it is our <u>collective character</u> that counts. It is America's will and internal strength;...our country was built by our <u>moral excellence</u>. Our current society needs an infusion of lasting character, to permeate our hearts and minds. We need to lead our lives with courage, pride, and purpose that generates from our character.

Life is a great adventure, and we are blessed to be living it in America. Live life with an open heart, mind, and soul. Be responsible for your attitude and beliefs. Expect the best from yourself and others. Accept and adapt to life's changes through making challenging choices. Stay your course. Instead of exclaiming "T.G.I.F." at the end of each week, be affirmative and begin each week with "T.G.I.M.",... "Thank God Its Monday!" Maintaining a positive attitude is my constant top priority. Our attitude filters and co-creates our outlook on life.

The powerful prose that follows (on the opposite page), written by Mother Teresa, entitled "Do It Anyway", inspires us to <u>transcend</u> despite the perception and behavior of others, to <u>achieve our purpose</u>...

People are often unreasonable.
Illogical and self-centered.
forgive them anyway.
If you are kind, people may accuse you of selfish,
Ulterior motives;
be kind anyway.
If you are successful, you will win some
False friends and some true friends;
succeed anyway.
If you are honest & frank, people may cheat you;
be honest and frank anyway.
What you spend years building,
Someone could destroy overnight;
build anyway.
If you find serenity and happiness,
They maybe jealous;
be happy anyway.
The good you do today,
People will often forget tomorrow;
do good anyway.
Give the world your best anyway.
You see, in the final analysis,
it is between you and God;
it was never between you and them anyway.

- MOTHER TERESA

LIFE IS GOOD. Transcend the moment...it's normal to have problems to solve. Always realize it's what *you do* with life's experiences and its challenging choices that really matters,...anyway. Make the most of life's invitations to grow!

Consider this challenge from George Bernard Shaw...

This is the true joy in life: The being used for a purpose recognized by yourself as a mighty one. The being a force of nature, instead of a feverish, selfish little clod of ailments and grievances complaining that the world will not devote itself to making you happy. I am of the opinion that my life belongs to the whole community, and as long as I live, it is my privilege to do for it whatever I can.

I want to be thoroughly used up when I die – for the harder I work, the more I live. I rejoice in life for its own sake. Life is no "brief candle" to me; it is a sort of splendid torch which I have got hold of for the moment, and I want to make it burn as brightly as possible before handing it on to future generations.

George Bernard Shaw
(1856 – 1950)
Irish dramatist, critic, and social reformer

I trust you found these quotes inspirational. To obtain maximum benefit from any cogent message, experience, or thought, we have to feel the emotional depth that gave rise to it.

Inspiration means to infuse by breathing in, to become full. We become influenced by being open, effortlessly permitting the flow to come in. Both require readiness and invitation, which are essential to embrace new experiences and discoveries. These are prerequisites for our most important discovery—ourselves. Total self-discovery enables us to find out who we are, our dreams, personal potential, our very own "magic" qualities.

Discovering self is a lifelong learning process of being able to be objective, hopeful, willful, courageous, committed, tenacious, self-accepting, proactive, creative, goal oriented, aware of self-made barriers, optimistic, able to shift paradigms, thinking inside, as well as outside the box, passionate, and persistent. We should strive to maintain an attitude to welcome the faces of life's realities and unexpected intrusions. We should see these as invitations to make challenging choices by filtering them through our mind, heart, and soul. Together, this triad synthesizes and creates the choice to employ. This process enables you to be your own best friend and enabler, by grabbing life by the horns. In a sense, the challenging choices you create, and the one you choose, is an application of your own "magic."

Remember life's decisions all have potential rewards and risks. To help with the difficult, complex ones, utilize this practical process used by Ben Carson, M.D., noted professor and neurosurgeon at Johns Hopkins University Medical Center. When faced with a tough decision, compare and contrast:

What are the best outcomes if I *do* this?
What are the worst outcomes if I *do* this?

With...

What are the best outcomes if I do *not* do this?
What are the worst outcomes if I do *not* do this?

Evaluate the results of your brainstorming on this juxtaposition to see what the potential risk- reward ratio might be. Decide by serious reflection.

This process, and outcome, is an example of coalescing our personal power to reach critical mass through our own mental, spiritual, and emotional fusion. This can be expressed in the following equation: $P = mse^3$, where P is personal power; mse^3 the integrated release of *mental, spiritual,* and *emotional* fusion, from our own potential energy. We achieve this by applying our positive attitude, being creative, seeking change, and using the force in our will.

If we don't change, we don't grow. If we don't grow, we aren't really living.

- Gail Sheehy

If we all did the things we are capable of doing, we would literally astound ourselves.

- Thomas A. Edison

Challenging Choices – Engaging Our Potential

Yes, life is complex
Continuous problems – issues to fix
Let these invitations be your guide
Which challenging choice to decide

Rather than become sour
Rely on personal power
Change your direction
With a new perception

Trust how you feel
Believe it will reveal
Be self-reliant
Become defiant

Gain in confidence
Go on the offense
So dig down deep
To generate a mighty feat!

To achieve mighty feats, generate a "bucket list" of new goals that will enhance your life. To assist with this challenge, the following section provides practical comprehensive "how to" prescriptions for continuous personal growth. I've utilized these self-help tools to enrich my life experiences and to strengthen my character. Remember, this mission is always a work in progress. We are all pilgrims on a life long journey. Together, by engaging our potential, we can co-create a better world. Let's go for it!

———————————●———————————

The difference between what we are doing and what we are capable of doing would solve most of the world's problems.

- Mahatma Gandhi

Holistic Prescriptions for Continuous Personal Growth

Sow an act, and you reap a habit. Sow a habit, and you reap a character. Sow a character, and you sow a destiny.

- Charles Reade

Nowadays some people expect the door of opportunity to be opened with a remote control.

- M Charles Wheeler

———————•———————

These prescriptions are for practices of daily living that will enhance your life. They are holistic, embracing personal management responsibilities for the continuous growth dimensions of perspective (spiritual), autonomy (mental), connectedness (social-emotional), and tone (physical).

Each prescription is to develop, apply, and maintain a skill. First is *knowledge*... understanding its' importance, power, and purpose at a deep level. Second is *attitude*, a strong optimistic desire to accomplish the end. Third is *proficiency*, being able to practice the skills on a daily basis to make it into a habit. *Together*, these skills empower you to value life, your life.

Life is a problem...it is our job to solve it. By applying these four dimensions of continuous growth, our mission becomes doable. Read and apply as needed. Take with or without food or water. Renew each month.

To personalize and maximize the benefit of these prescriptions, as you read and reflect on them, pay attention to any that you connect with. Use them to open the door to sincere introspection that identifies a need for change and growth in; things you do (internal) that make you less effective than you can be, and things others do, (external) that make you less effective. Use this food for thought to identify new goals and skills for increased effectiveness and personal power. Prioritize your insights to choose the most important one(s) with which to begin.

Next, generate your own prescription that will achieve your desired outcome(s). Make your written script specific, goal oriented, practical, doable, and meaningful. When finished with your final draft, sign your name at the bottom, adding the initials SP.D. (doctor of self-power) after your signature. This mindset applies the same magical metaphors the Wizard of Oz uses to empower the lion, scarecrow, and tin man to actualize traits they already had, but didn't believe in. It validates the potential of your script and empowers you to do it. Conceive, believe, and achieve.

Pledge to achieve your prescription by making it into a habit. Release your focused, determined personal power, to walk your talk. This prescription process should be empowering and challenging. Plan your work, and work your plan.

Over fifty years as a teacher, school administrator, college professor, husband, father, and friend, I've found the following qualities and practices keys for success.

Holistic Prescriptions for Continuous Personal Growth by Category

Physical – Tone

Practice Wellness – Our society and culture promotes the pleasure principle. We are bombarded with commercials to eat, drink, and be merry. As a consequence, we develop poor health habits and weak self-discipline. The antidote to this influence is to practice wellness, maximizing the quality of your life physically, mentally, socially, spiritually, and emotionally. Wellness means to care enough about yourself;...to care for yourself. To maintain a healthy, balanced life requires a conscious commitment to excellence. By implementing a personal plan you "sharpen your saw" everyday. Practicing wellness preserves and enhances the greatest asset you have—*You*.

While knowledge is power, it does not cause empowerment. You must commit to a wellness plan and stick with it. The poet Kahlil Gibran reminds us, "Sayings remain meaningless unless they are embodied in habit." We have to walk our talk. Examine your lifestyle and health status. You are the one responsible for much of your health. By improving your lifestyle behaviors, you can improve your health, energy, and outlook on life. When you awaken, do you say, "Good Morning, Lord", or, "Good Lord, it's morning."

Take Care of Your Temple – Your body is your temple. Value, worship, and develop habits that maintain and nurture your physical self. Monitor your weight, blood pressure, heart rate, significant blood factors, especially triglycerides, cholesterol, glucose, etc. Manage stress. Develop resiliency.

We are what we eat and drink. Include more fruits, vegetables (multicolored), and grains in your healthy, purposeful diet. Eat less sugar, salt, and fats. Drink more water (experts say eight glasses a day). Include health promoting vitamins, minerals, fish oil (omega 3 rich), antioxidants, and other supplements that work for your age and physical needs.

Personalize your own fitness program. Include exercises in endurance, flexibility, and strength. Maintain a regimen for a half hour or more, four to five times each week. Do activities you enjoy. Vary your routines and change when needed. Variety is the spice of life.

Your fitness goal should be to develop and sustain endurance and perseverance. Renew yourself. Stay your course.

Mental – Autonomy

Be Creative – Analyze problems and procedures to see if there is a new and better way of dealing with them. Get "out of the box" of the normal habits, pathways, policies, and expectations. Dare to be different. Experiment. Trail blaze!

Be Where You Are: Stay in the Here and Now – While it is important to learn from the past and plan for the future, we can let our energy and focus be fixed on either. We need to be in the present, to enjoy the here and now. The grass is not greener someplace else; it's where you fertilize it. This is true of time. If we regret and want to relive the past, we miss opportunities in front of us. If we defer a happy existence by waiting for some future event, we deny the power that can exist in our present environment. Remember that yesterday and tomorrow are twin thieves that rob us of today. Carpe diem. Get out of automatic pilot and into paying full attention. Use your mind with purposeful attention. Be fully aware of the present moment.

Anticipate and Initiate – Be proactive. Plan ahead to be ready before problems overcome you. Take actions early so you are in control and not in crisis. Spend your thoughtful time before and not after, when it's too late. The three keys to success in teaching (and parenting) are preparation, preparation, and preparation.

Learn and Grow Each Day – Life is a continuous learning experience. Expand and stretch your mind. Learn from your mistakes, and increase your vision daily. Be open to new insights, but don't be so liberal minded that your brains fall out. Use your mind wisely. Don't develop psycho-sclerosis (narrowing of the mind). Maintain rational rather than irrational thoughts. No "mind farts."

Part of the learning-growth process is unlearning and relearning. Much of what we've been taught is obsolete and inaccurate. The world is not fixed. Black and white coexist as numerous shades of gray. Filter information and synthesize your own reality.

Yogi Berra was right on when he said, "If you come to a fork in the road, take it." Adapt your mental maps to the new terrain that appears around us each day. The information-communication flow through cyberspace requires much reflection and re-education. Replace your "software programs" often, to be on the cutting edge of new realities. Apply your wisdom gained from being buffeted by life and with your ethereal will. Life is not either or, one way. God maybe a s/he, not just male. Look for complex in the simple and the simple in the complex. It's all there. Isn't it?

Let Go And Let God – Transcend your ego. Forget your hurts. Want and get your mind and soul into a better space. If you hold onto and let fester a hurt, anger, or resentment, it will devour you. Forgive and forget. Holding a grudge against someone is like taking poison and waiting for that person to die. What you focus on expands. Elbert Hubbard reminds us that,...God will not look us over for medals, degrees, and diplomas, but for scars.

Keep Your Power - Do not permit yourself to become addicted, albeit to food, shopping, sex, alcohol, tobacco, drugs, relationships, cyberspace, etc. Addiction is when you give control over to whatever it is you feel you must have. Get high on life. Maintain balance. Be the master of your destiny and health. Keep your power, and – do not surrender to the devils (addictions).

Accept and Manage Stress – We can't control stressors and many external events that occur in our lives. But we can manage these to lessen our reactions to them. Apply the "Richter Scale of Stress" when you feel yourself being carried away by life's bumps in the road. Most distress is brought about by our own perception (interpretations) of external events. Through cognitive distortion (a.k.a. magnification) we turn a small event into a major stressor. So the point is, to control your reactions to neutral events and keep them where they belong. Avoid "Stinkin thinkin"– mind farts. Remember, what you focus on,...<u>EXPANDS</u>.

Use Discernment – Suspend Judgment – Sometimes it is better to ignore, than react to a minor event. Overlooking a minor infraction or misbehavior by a child (even your own), especially if it occurs in a group setting, may save the day. By focusing on your chagrin and negative emotion at the moment, you may behave toward the "perpetrator" in a manner that escalates the "problem," by embarrassing the child, and giving the other children something to cheer about. By remaining in neutral, you maintain control. You can always talk to the child about his behavior later in private, which is more effective than embarrassment in front of their peers. Not to decide - is to decide.

Be Flexible, Go with the Flow, Expect the Unexpected — Remember life is what happens when you are busy planning something else; also, life's unfinished. Leave room in your daily work schedule for the UNEXPECTED. Find and pursue the meaning, mission, and purpose of your life. You do not manage time; you manage *yourself*. By soul-searching, we realize who we are and what our journey is. The *meaning of life* is found by making the most of the meaning you give to your life and others. The question to ask is not what is the meaning of life, but what is the meaning of <u>*my*</u> life?

Stay The Course ... But Be Flexible

Maintain Balance — We all lead busy lives. Twenty-four hours seems inadequate for what has to be accomplished in our frenetic day. Yet, ironically, it's not more time that we need.

Time management is a misnomer. We do not manage time; we manage ourselves. Our goal is to keep a balance of what demands our time (non-negotiable) and where we want to use it (negotiable or controllable). To help master personal management skills, apply this concept/tool. Start by doing an inventory of how and where you spend your time in an average week. At the end of each day, write down what you were doing every fifteen minutes in each hour (do all twenty-four). Analyze and categorize each fifteen-minute segment into these four major areas:

Work - Formal and informal, include work you bring home or do at home (cooking, cleaning, child rearing, chores, etc.).

Maintenance — Sleeping, medical upkeep, exercising, etc. Also include how much time you spend maintaining your support systems (calling or visiting friends, nurturing relationships), practicing your religion, spiritual nourishment, meditating, reading, planning, prioritizing, learning, etc.

Fun, Play, Amusement — Going to the movies, library, museums, enjoying sports, hobbies, or other personal interests that give you joy.

Free Sense — Activities that activate your senses, experiencing nature, listening to music, making love, experiencing rapture, etc. Total the amount of time you spent in each category. There are 168 hours in a week. How much time are you spending in all four areas? Are you utilizing your 168 hours in a balanced manner? Are you investing yourself into the values and priorities that are meaningful to you? Become committed to say "yes" and "no" to what's most important to you and yours. Whose agenda are you following?

Develop Self Discipline and Self Love for Stability — To maintain a sense of positive self-esteem, we must accept responsibility for self-discipline and self-love. We tend to make ourselves feel unimportant by listening to our inner critic, our innate ability to judge and evaluate subjectively, negatively, and severely. We destroy our own self-esteem by our own negative self-talk (cognitive distortions) and subsequent bad feeling. But feeling bad; does not mean we are bad; they are uncomfortable messages to be understood, so we can remedy them by reflection and the power of positive, objective thinking. We actually learn from our feeling of low self-esteem. Self-esteem waxes and wanes; it is not constant. Feeling "low" self-esteem is feedback to our ego of blame and guilt because we know we should do better. It is a dynamic, complex process of perceptions, interpretations, and integrations into our value system. A change in situation, belief about success, or lack of goal orientation, causes us to lose faith in ourselves.

Self-esteem, by itself, is not enough. Just as your shadow is not you, how you feel about yourself is not you. We own our feelings, not vice versa. It is up to us to regulate and understand the process of self-esteem, which is part psychology of adaptation, positive philosophy, resiliency, character, wisdom, and faith. We cast the shadow; the shadow does not cast us.

Remember that self esteem is but one dimension of the complex human spirit that we need to totally embrace and use in our journey. The true measure of our self-worth is to improve our character, competence, perseverance, and optimism. This maintains stability.

Social – Emotional – Connectedness

Lessen Control – There is very little in life we really control. Realize that during our experience here in life school, we only rent. We do not take anything with us when we leave. If you let your need to be in control become obsessive its force will cripple you with worry and anxiety. Differentiate between what you can, and cannot control. Remember that more, often turns out to be less, while less, is actually more.

Love – A lot. Love is far more than a word(s). Love is a verb. Love is action. Love transcends ego and negative feelings or memories. It has power and mystery. When you're feeling hurt, disappointed, or angry with another person, that is the time you must break through those barriers you are creating to reach out to that person. Love has great power when we let it work. I know first-hand forgiving is very hard to do. It doesn't require the other person to do anything, and you have to give everything. That's just the point—*forgive* means *for giving* (of yourself). Go beyond. Transcend. Love is action. Create change. Love is magic. Remember to love *yourself*. Be your own best friend. Be aware of your self-talk. Use discernment in choosing your words. "I need to practice that more" rather than "I'm terrible at that."

Divest Yourself of Roles – You cannot not be a father, teacher, principal, etc., if you have that role. Others dealing with you are always conscious of your role(s), so you can "die to yourself' and forget your ego, your formal role(s), your need for power or control, you get them from outside. Get down on your knees, sit on the floor, cry, and hug, go with whatever it takes to connect with where the other person is. Be spontaneous, playful, and childlike, when needed. Be in the moment. Forget your agenda and yourself, and be the other person. You'll never be perceived as being weak. Actually, by "dying" to yourself, you become more alive and appreciated by the other person. You are always the roles you have. They do not go away because you think, "I'm acting out of role." Do what the moment and reality call for.

Value Your Job – No matter what it is. Value your work. There were many times I hated my work. The "in" basket seemed to never be empty, and you seldom got a compliment, just petty complaints. Your job enables you to work with other people and is a support system for the mission of your job. It wasn't until I retired, that I really learned to value my job, and I realized, after trying to get work as a consultant, or teach a course, that you had to hustle for everything. You have to create and make work. When you have a job, the work is waiting for you each day. You don't have to make it happen; it's there. Value your job. Be thankful for it. Look forward to going to, and being at work. It is one of life's gifts.

Lead a Rich Personal and Professional Life – So much of our lives, our work lives, are in a social arena. Usually we are solving other people's problems and having to please others. After a while, if all you do is deal with paper, problems, and politics, you get dull. The antidote to this is personal growth. Do things that give your life meaning, purpose, and are fun for *you*. Have hobbies and interests, and actively pursue them. Be passionate about something *other* than work. Spend time by yourself walking, listening to your favorite music, or meditating. Prayer is you talking to God; meditation is God talking to you. Go to nature often. Walk in the woods or on a beach...twelve months of the year. Some of my most relaxing and enjoyable moments in nature have been in the winter or in the rain. Ask yourself this question once a month: am I living to work: or working to live? You have to make yourself happy. Maintain balance.

Accept and Embrace Change – Change is the only constant. Your mindset, experience, or paradigm is limited. Be willing to shift your paradigms about work or life frequently, or reality and opportunities, will pass you by. Nothing stays the same. Adapt. Change as needed. Be flexible. Yet maintain your priorities and principles.

Be Humble – No matter what college degree, fame, or job title you have, if it wasn't for other people and their problems, your job probably wouldn't exist. Remember it's *normal* to have problems. Recognize and learn from your mistakes and moments of hubris. Grow.

Empower Others – Help others solve their own problems. Do not rescue people. That disempowers them. Only go 50 percent of the way (at most) in helping. Once you go beyond 50 percent not only are you rescuing the person, but if he or she doesn't follow your advice, or you regret the amount of time he or she is taking from you, you will begin to resent the other person. Remember, who owns the problem? That's the person that has to understand it and find his or her own solutions.

Delegate – Don't do it all yourself. This is an area with which I needed help. We tend to want to be in control, in charge, and to micromanage others. The more we delegate, with the authority to do it, the more we create loyalty, and trust. It also lets us spend more time listening, observing, planning, and correcting (leadership activities), rather than managing. Delegating releases creativity and ownership in the other person who assumes responsibility.

Be Human – Listen, especially with your eyes (nonverbal cues) and your heart (empathy, but not sympathy). Words are only part of the message. Look for, and feel the clues that express where the other person's energy is (or isn't). Is he or she focused, in perspective, in reality, or caught up in anxieties or fantasies? Validate those feelings. Accept where the person is. Be emotionally available to them (open). Bond. Connect.

It's Normal to Have Problems – Life would not be challenging if there were no problems, difficult issues, concerns, and crises. It would be abnormal not to be buffeted by them. Accept and solve them. Instead of being reactive, be proactive by applying the solution or fix that benefits you and others, before the crisis. Stay in control. There are two Chinese characters that represent the word crisis—danger and opportunity. <u>Always look for the silver lining</u> and seize the moment creatively.

The Importance of Training – Children, whether your own or borrowed (students), need to be trained very much like a puppy. Behavioral standards and expectations have to be reinforced, so they become automatic. You must set the stage with the quality of character you expect and demand the same. Explain your insistence in the context of the *"us"*, *"we"* and *"togetherness"* of a close-knit family that shows each other constant respect, attention, and concern. Our objectives are to help each other, not to work against one another. Be specific with your instructions and constantly reinforce them. "I like the way you asked for that first, before taking it." I like the way you held the door open. "That was nice to let John go ahead of you." Remember, kids are watching every verbal and nonverbal communication you make. Your consistent role modeling of respect, dignity, honesty, manners, and care is essential. The culture (learned behavior) you create and maintain pays off. Your influence becomes silent, but is felt, like gravity. Training is equally important to teaching knowledge and skills, and must come first. Children need to know that you are the parent, and students that you are the teacher, not a playmate. First things, first. Process has to precede content (subject matter). Children need to pay attention. Proper behavior must be constant and automatic, not situational.

Communicating a Problem – When it is necessary to communicate a problem, concern, or issue to a child or adult, be sure it contains these parts. Be specific as to the nature or cause of the problem. Avoid global statements like, "John is having difficulty reading." Do some diagnosis and prescribing: "John will be a more effective reader if he improves his comprehension skills. I suggest you read stories to him and ask questions about their meaning. Help him draw out conclusions. Have him read to you and ask him to explain what the author was writing about."

If you must present a personal problem (health, behavioral, evidence or strong suspicion of alcohol, tobacco or drug use, depression, suicidal ideation, etc.), always accompany the problem with written information about where to go to get help, counseling support, or therapy. This information should be about local professional, organizations, and agencies with addresses and phone numbers. Hope must be given along with the anxiety. If you offer a diagnosis, then provide where to go to get the treatment or cure. And remember, who owns the problem?

Develop Many Strategies and New Solutions to problems — Antony Jay states, "The uncreative mind can spot wrong answers but it takes a creative mind to spot wrong questions."

Be creative. Remember Abraham Maslow's observation: "If the only tool you have is a hammer, then you see every problem as a nail." To do so is to remain in first order change—staying within the system that itself remains unchanged. There are times we need to bring about second order change —changing the system itself (change of change). Albert Einstein reminds us "no problem can be solved from the same consciousness that created it." To effect second-order change, we need to follow a process (best with a team) that has a clear definition of the issue-problem, or goal, in concrete terms, investigates solutions attempted to date, develops a clear definition of the concrete changes desired (outcomes), and formulates and implements a specific and detailed plan to produce this change. There are times we cannot do things alone.

Be One Way with the Group, But Multiple Ways with Individuals – When you are playing a role (parent, teacher, coach, etc.) with a group (family, class, team), you need consistent, congruent communication. The group has to learn the key expectations and habits that you, as leader, expect. You do not have time to individualize meaning. When it is necessary to personalize your attention and communicate with an individual in the group, de-role yourself and connect with that person through his or her unique personality. You can sense whether to be softer or tougher, patient or urgent, etc. The individual, one-on-one communication needs to create a bond and acceptance between both parties. Let your guard down and understand that role has many facets to it. Show you care. Listen. Coach. Wear one mask in front of the group, but wear many working one to one. It's okay to be different one on one. You can be relaxed and be you, not a fixed role.

Be Passionate – Develop and nurture a passion about some aspect of life. Stay passionate with whatever this might be: a sport, hobby, charity, service to others, volunteering, listening to music, enjoying nature, etc. We need to spend private time to create and maintain meaning, enjoyment, and purpose in our lives, and others. Experiencing passion keeps us lubricated with positive energy. Passion keeps us balanced and in love with life. Apply the mission-motto of the Navy Seabees: **"Can Do"**. Dispel ennui. Discover and sing your "heart's song" each day.

Promote Intergenerational Awareness and Understanding – Because of the rapidity and constant change in the gut level values we develop in American society and culture, generation gaps can also cause communication gaps. Today's senior citizens, as an example, are more cautious with spending money, have strict belief systems, are accustomed to a slower pace, and "old-fashioned" use of the few technology devices introduced during their lifetime. *We, us,* family, and God, were important values to live by, and still are.

Compare that worldview with that of today's youth. Steeped in instant gratification, instant electronic communication through cell phones, iPods, and cyberspace, their emphasis from their conditioning imprints is much different than their grandparents, and even parents. *Me, I,* and *my friends,* are paramount. Paradoxically parents tend to adapt to their children, rather than the children adjusting to their parent's expectations.

Commonly shared values are few and far between. Yet, we cannot say that today's youth are indifferent to the world or to us older adults, just different. Yes, the world we now share is different. It requires us to accept flux and change as normal, not abnormal. Much greater understanding of each other is needed. We need to transcend our view of reality to create a shared view with our youth. Shared meaning becomes a process of listening, accepting, and even changing what we consider as normal. The twenty-first century requires unlearning, as well as new learning, greater use of patience and new vision. Being different doesn't mean we have to differ. Seek first to understand the other person's point of view. Wait to share your perspective, then by thinking a win-win outcome, we synthesize. Listen more. Take time. Go with the flow. Adjust and adapt.

Expand Your Comfort Zone - We all like to live our lives in what is commonly referred to as our "comfort zone". We feel secure and safe when we're there. Yet, this zone can become a cocoon that prevents new and needed experiences for personal growth. Be aware engineers call the comfort zone the "*dead zone*". Using a thermostat as a metaphor, they point out that our preferred temperature for our comfort level, once set, maintains that temperature. If it gets warmer, the thermostat lowers the temperature, and if the ambient air gets colder, it raises the temperature. The "comfort zone", the temperature we set for ourselves is really a "dead zone", for if the temperature remains constant, <u>nothing happens</u>. Life has highs and lows continuously, and our comfort zone has to be wide and flexible to accept reality.

Be sure you don't develop an attitude that you are like the thermostat that controls and regulates automatically your narrow personal preferences. Teddy Roosevelt was right when he stated, "Far better is it to dare mighty things than to rank with those poor spirits who enjoy much nor suffer much."

Be Humorous - See humor in situations, laugh at them, and laugh at yourself. Don't take life too seriously. Lighten up. See the positive. It's there all around us. Remember that laughter is inner jogging, and it diffuses stress. Laugh often and hard. Start your day by reading the funnies or comic strips, first. Keep the smile on your face and attitude all day!

Maintain a Support System - Life can be very abandoning and lonely, especially at trying times. It's essential to have a support system in place to help you pass through the dark clouds. Nurture and value your best friend(s). They are your "go-to" guys in time of need, and vice versa. Communicate frequently to maintain a close and constant relationship. Friendship is a priceless gift, wind beneath your wings.

At the same time, become and rely on being your own best friend. Nurture and love yourself. This reciprocal relationship of acceptance and love will help sustain you. Be your strongest supporter. See my poem "Thanks, Best Friends", (pg. 166).

Perspective – Spiritual

Be Optimistic and Positive – American culture focuses on the negative. All American babies, in addition to getting a social security number, receive a Ph.D. in negative evaluation at birth. We constantly get feedback about what we didn't do, or did wrong. Playing blemish and scapegoat hunting are America's favorite sports. We need to overcome the negative inner voice that we were given by our parents, teachers, peers, and especially the perfect media images. Be your own coach. Praise and encourage yourself and others. Be your own cheerleader. I'd rather be an optimist who's wrong, than a pessimist who's right. Make deposits in your own emotional bank account so there are more than the withdrawals you or others make. The formula for successful parenting is four parts praise, and one part pruning. Be careful and sparing with criticism. The term "constructive criticism" is the ultimate oxymoron.

View Life As A Gift — Embrace each day, even with its problems, and not feeling well. Want what you have, rather than having what you want. Maintain a positive attitude on life.

There are so many people born with less normal physical qualities than you, that cannot do the things you do, and take for granted. And you never know which day, minute, or moment maybe your last (or your loved one's). Make every day Thanksgiving, accepting and embracing each day as a gift, with gratitude.

Grow in Wisdom – Ben Franklin astutely observed that "common sense is not so common." Knowledge and wisdom are both needed. Knowledge is about learning facts and information. If we remain superficial about knowledge, it does not give us much power. Remember that being able to verbalize an answer to a question does not mean or demonstrate we understand the words we are using. Knowledge is means, and wisdom is ends. Further, with the rapidity of new information available each day, we have to keep current with emerging, viable facts. We need to evaluate fact with its value.

Wisdom helps us apply knowledge in a prudent manner and consider the possible cause and effect relationships. By applying discernment, judgment, and filtering outcomes, we use wisdom to make appropriate, beneficial decisions. Wisdom transcends information, synthesizing information with the application of realistic outcomes from all known variables. Wisdom even tells us to get uncomfortable not knowing, but to be open minded and receptive to new ideas. We need to remain focused, and committed to life, with a philosophical framework that interprets our personal experiences with meaning and hope, even in life's seemingly hopeless moments. Walk on. Grow. Increase your vision.

Increase Your Vision...and Mind Set - The world we live in is not a simple duality of good or bad, black or white, opposites. Apply the wisdom and understanding of the Yin/Yang symbol from Chinese philosophy. Prevent the "Tyranny of the OR" – usual rational thinking that cannot easily accept paradox, understand that two seemingly contradictory forces or ideas can exist simultaneously. The "Tyranny of OR" is the belief that things have to be A or B, but not both. The Yin/Yang symbolizes co-existence.

Liberate your mind set with the "Genius of the AND" – the ability to accept <u>both</u> extremes of a number of reality dimensions at the same time. Instead of only choosing <u>between</u> A or B, figure out a way to have A <u>and</u> B. This requires transcendence and synthesis. To paraphrase F. Scott Fitzgerald – the test of first-rate intelligence is the ability to hold two opposing ideas in the mind at the same time. and still retain the ability to function. The emerging world we live in requires this creative – adaptive – flexible – interactive mind set.

Find "*Realigion*" – Webster's defines religion as: a service, worship, commitment, observance, scrupulous conformity, system of beliefs held with ardor and faith, personal or institutionalized. Is your religion internally (personal) or externally (institutionalized) based?

Are you conscious of moral gravity, while unseen, is felt by you constantly? Do you see yourself as part of a higher plane, an external dimension that gives your life meaning and purpose?

Spirituality is natural and God given. Religion is man made. Both are necessary components, enabling us to generate love for our self and others. For religion to be effective, it should not be experienced only behind stained glass windows on Saturday or Sunday mornings, or holidays, but everyday. Religions tend to be an impersonal affair, remaining superficial with loyalty to the institution rather than to personal responsibility to let God's presence manifest and act through us.

"Realigion" is living a spiritually driven, inner-directed life that stays focused, faithful to a personal knowledge and love of God. It can be aided by religion if it strengthens you to stay committed. Too often, however, religious rituals and repetitious routines do not inspire or motivate self-responsibility for experiencing God.

Our love of God and ourselves is a continuous, personal progressive revelation. By embedding faith, hope, and love in our conscious mind, heart, and soul, we find "*Realigion.*" This internally autonomous value system results from releasing the Holy Spirit that dwells inside everyone and guides us during our journey through earth school.

Maintain a Positive Attitude – Be cognizant on how you are interpreting your life. It is imperative that we maintain a positive, purposeful, optimistic outlook and focus on our goals. Our attitude is the compass that keeps our life's mission and purpose on course. It is the spiritual catalyst that generates courage. A positive attitude is everything. Apply the sage advice of Katherine Mansfield: Could we change our attitude, we should not only see life differently, but life itself would come to be different.

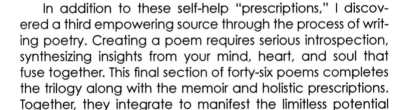

In addition to these self-help "prescriptions," I discovered a third empowering source through the process of writing poetry. Creating a poem requires serious introspection, synthesizing insights from your mind, heart, and soul that fuse together. This final section of forty-six poems completes the trilogy along with the memoir and holistic prescriptions. Together, they integrate to manifest the limitless potential power we all have within us. We need to <u>truly believe in ourselves and our own ability to co-create reality</u>.

Few really believe. The most only believe that they believe or even make believe.

-John Lancaster Spalding

EMPOWERING POETRY

The psychological mechanism used by grace to raise us to prayer is the same that puts in movement the poetic experience.

- Henri Bremond

Poetry ennobles the heart and eyes, and unveils the meaning of all things upon which the heart and the eyes dwell. It discovers the secret rays of the universe, and restores us to forgotten paradises.

- Dame Edith Sitwell

Poetry is simply the most beautiful, impressive, and effective mode of saying things.

- Mathew Arnold

Webster's defines a poem as creating the sense of a complete emotional response through meaning, sound, and rhythm. From my experience as an amateur poet, this response comes from a deep spiritual or philosophical personal experience. The event changes something inside you. Over time, your unconscious and conscious mind distills the profound effects on you; like brandy becoming cognac. The poet's chosen words become the frames in time-lapse photography, each one empowering us to see and create the experience of a rose bud unfolding into maturity, by transcending and synthesizing a new reality.

The final expression releases itself as a poem, empowering, I hope, the reader as much as the poet. It is an end state of a long birth process, requiring reflection and continuous editing to get it right. I trust you will be empowered by reading these poems, as I was in writing them to share with you, through our common human spirit. Poetry is magical, **increasing our vision** of the marvel and majesty of life. Their topics include: Nature, Time, Contemporary American Society and Culture, Sports, Feelings, and Spiritual-Philosophical.

Cliff's Poems

Reflections of Synthesis and Transcendence

EMPOWERING POETRY

NATURE

<u>UNDERWATER REEF</u>

In this quiet, secret, rainbow world
Of smooth, easy motion
Where is the traffic?
Where are the cars?
I expect this beauty
To be a mirage

<u>NATURE</u>

Is it the green in the trees
Or the warm breeze
Sunlight shimmering
Or waves splashing

Whatever the season
Splendor awaits
Outdoors, free
For all to enjoy

Watch squirrels playing
Leaves falling
Streams flowing
Clouds Changing

At last, Quite
True silence, how loud
Will surely fix this hole
I've made in my soul

SPRUCE TREE BEAUTY

Greenish-blue, softly standing
Your graceful branches bend
Sloping gently down, down
No spaces to be found
From top to ground
Soon you'll cast a magic glow
Completely covered by winter's snow

LONELY CLOUD

Where did you begin?
Where have you been?
Where are you going?
I ask the sky
But get no reply

NATURE'S WISHES

It shouldn't take a hurricane
Or tornado spout
To put us in
Our place

Look at tides
Changing beaches
Broken branches
Swollen rivers

Read – these signs
And those in us
Nature's wishes
Come true

DOG (GOD SPELLED BACKWARDS)

Always giving unconditional love
Bringing peace, like a dove
Accepting, listening, faithful
Anxiously awaiting my return

Breed doesn't matter
They all flatter
Mess they must
And make a fuss

That bark tells me
It's time for a walk
Four-legged best friend
You help me mend

PRECIOUS PRESENCE

Slowly as I approach this quiet tranquil pond
So does a splendid outstretched Blue Heron
Gliding in low, landing softly in the water's edge tall grass
Hoping to feed on minnow, carp, or bass.

With all its splendor and sonar feet
That have already found a fish, flipped into it's beak
At the end of a magical curved neck fit
That instantly straightens like a lightning whip.

Now it moves on, with a slow, careful, patient pace
Walking cautiously, ready, poised with grace
Stopping frequently, standing motionless, searching to find
Always relaxed, displaying elegance and pride.

So captured, I pleadingly pray
Please God, let it stay, not fly away
I want to enjoy and completely capture
To maintain this moment of Blue Heron Rapture.

ON A LATE FALL WALK IN THE FOREST

I stop on a carpet of leaves
To stare up from the ground
Amongst these naked trees
To admire one I've found

There's one lonely leaf on its' highest branch
Captured, I join in its' private trance
Hoping it will fall off now,
Performing a ballet dance

Gracefully fluttering down
To a new location
Joining its' brethren
Anticipating a winter vacation.

LONG ISLAND'S TREASURES

East to West beaches bask in continuous daylight sun
Perfect for swimming, wading, relaxing, or just fun
Ocean waves rhythmically break, roll in and out, leaving
sandy trails
Many harbors and bays beckon for spreading sails.

Focus your mind on the effect of time and tidal variation
Subtly, silently, unveiling or covering your renovated
location
Tour the unique East Island branches
Capture the essence of vineyards and mansions.

Explore the Hampton's beaches on crisp autumn days
Oceans placid, people free, blue skies, no haze
Search through waves' wash for shells and weathered glass
Rapture at the clean sand, dunes, and tall grass.

Encounter a varied itinerary
Visit Fire Island via bridge or ferry
Explore nature's diversity at Morton Wildlife Refuge on
Peconic Bay
Drive to Montauk Point to share a delightful day.

Savor the specter of Indian summer
Fall weather morphing, listening to a different drummer
But north winds turns colder, which winter does bring
Once active golf courses now sleep, awaiting the promise
of spring.

MONTAUK POINT BEACH TRANSFORMATIONS

Rather than visit Montauk Point for just a few hours in your day
Plan to go when the weather will change, and stay
Sunup to sunset, savoring each breath of salt waters scent
Behold Atlantic's vastness, appearing to have no horizon
Waves constantly unfolding, rolling up and down on wet sand

Watch ocean breezes make dune grasses bend, and sway
Soon to strengthen, morphing wave ends into froth and spray
Frenzied seagulls struggle to fly, quiet, to let winds pass by
Tomorrow, with calm winds, airborne they'll try To reach billowing cumulus clouds in a clear blue sky

Walk slowly along ocean's edge, observing fiddler crabs scurrying sideways for a place to park
Seaweed washing in, piling higher, stopping at high tides mark
Listen to wind and waves converge, orchestrating into a roar
Together as a team, pounding gravel and shells into shore
Yet, later, forgiving, caressing, producing a hard sandy floor

While surf casting is fun, before you go swimming...
Study surface water for signs of undertow or rip tides beginning
Respect waves, ocean's power, better observed from a distance
And best of all, return in fall, when beaches are empty
Ocean's placid, waters still warm, and parking is easy

A "MIRACLE" FROM MOTHER NATURE

Sitting in an oak tree deer stand twelve feet high
Cold, alert, hoping for a buck to come by
Suddenly, visiting with a flourish, is a chickadee
Landing on a branch right next to me

His penetrating eyes ask, why are you here?
If you're looking down for a deer?
He's inquisitive, cute, compact perfection
Intensely facing in my direction

Now, jumping, happily hopping in a forward dance
Staring me down, putting me into a trance
I can't take my eyes off him
My concentration in hunting has become dim

Abruptly, after a short flight, he lands on my hat
I feel him there, though he didn't look fat
Bending over my hat's brim, looking at me upside down!
Still figuring out why I'm not on the ground

I didn't get a deer that season
Yet, I'll never forget it, for this reason
A marvelous chickadee experience from her
A "miracle" from the majesty of mother nature

RAINBOW ECSTASY

Gaze at a rainbow formation
Nature's unpredictable unique creation
Such absolute, symmetrical precision
Just elegant, simple, painted perfection.

TIME

MYSTICAL MAGICIAN

How can time
Steady, absolute
Clock sure
Vanish so?

When I'm with you
An hour's a minute!
Magically dissolving
Instantly, invisibly

Oh, time enemy
Be my friend!
Reverse your trick
Make a minute last an hour

And when you can't…
Help me hear
Your presence pass
To know you were really here.

DREAM – DAY AND NIGHT

Since I dream at night
Why not at day?
Active minds have twins
Named conscious and unconscious
Which must function free
Besides, day dreaming
Brings delight to me!

DESTINY

The criteria of time
Weeks, months, and years
Applies a clock, a calendar
Man's inventions of reality

It's really the cycles and seasons
That give us reasons
That shape and mold us
Like rain on rock

Beating, slowly, rapidly
Carving what is destined
Can we measure
What isn't finished yet?

THE GOLDEN YEARS

What golden years?
All I shed is tears
From my new friends
Arthur Itus, Ann Gina, and Charlie Horse.

Where's the gold?
That's what I was told.
Has to be a myth
I'm downing another fifth.

Oh, joy to the metallic age
Gold in my teeth,
Silver in my hair,
And lead in my butt.

Just another phase
From passing days
To hell with no pain,
No gain.

At least my urine's gold
Or so I'm told.
See, I'm not so old
Just in the senior citizen fold.

MEMORIES OF MY MEMORY

As the years fly by so fast,
I often wonder if I had a past?
I know I had many fond recollections
To which I can't seem to make connections

Now, I go into a room
And then ask why?
Did I come here
To catch a fly?

Where did I park?
Wait a minute
Did I drive far?
Do I even own a car?

See, I've already misplaced this poem
Has to be here at home.
Where should I go looking?
Oh God, am I supposed to be cooking?

As frustrating as it is
There's still hope
At least I can remember
I forgot something, just not what.

So next time I forget
I will not fret,
I'm still all me,
Just with less memory.

<u>GET WITH IT!</u>

This world is changing so fast
I seem to have no relevant past
Change is so constant and steady
I don't know how to be ready.

Up seems down, down is up
I'm caught on a speed bump
My own worst enemy,
Not being in the twenty-first century.

<u>TIME... FRIEND OR FOE?</u>

How precious, ready and free
Yet, where does it flee?
Never seems to be enough
Using it up on unimportant stuff.

Ignore others demands
Conflicting with your plans
As good as their requests may seem
They'll take away your dream.

When you know what you must do
Life's easier to pursue
Your highest priorities you must find
By filtering in your heart and mind.

Stay your course
Be your own boss
Know what's important to defend
By managing yourself, time's your friend.

CONTEMPORARY AMERICAN SOCIETY AND CULTURE

ENOUGH GRAY HAIR!

What happened to civility?
Individualized and group responsibility?
All we get from the media
Is constant negativity.

Let's change direction
How about some reflection
Perspective and correction
To celebrate all that is good around us.

We need hope,
Not despair
I already have
Enough gray hair.

<u>DRIVING'S NOT LIKE IT USED TO BE</u>

When I first learned to drive
Everything seemed just fine
No road rage or blasting horn
A new breed of drivers has been born.

Now I dread to take the wheel `
Cause I know how I'll feel
True, my car is high tech
But I'm a nervous wreck.

I fear for my life
How do I protect my wife?
Don't drive into my trunk
Is that driver drunk?

A car is a new haven for self-basking
Drivers involved in multitasking
Auto insurance rates are rising
Should not be surprising.

We need to return to practicality
Driving manners, obeying laws, civility
Using patience, courtesy and common sense
To stop this highway stress.

<u>OUR WARPED WORLDVIEW</u>

Why are crime, wars, and violence in favor?
Seemingly the sole focus of TV, magazines, and my
newspaper.
Our world is not just hate and sorrow
There are good deeds we need to hear about from
yesterday, today, and tomorrow.

We need to increase our vision
To include daily human love, support and courage
That exists consistently, in all places
To replace fear with a smile on our faces.

Ours NEWS must be balanced
With every bad story, share a good one
Focus on the positive that's all around us
No need to create negative fuss.

<u>CREDIT CARD NOOSE TIGHTENING?</u>

Before you reach in your wallet to cover your bash
Think, do I have the necessary cash?
Is what you're buying a need or a want?
For your credit card will surely help your money to part.

Hold back that habit of instant gratification
For you may not soon be able to afford a vacation.
What you haven't paid for today will bring sorrow
For you will be paying off your interest many a tomorrow.

U.S. CONGRESS — THE DYSFUNCTIONAL BRANCH

Progress is our most important product G.E. used to
proclaim
This slogan heard over and over
Led to their fame.
What progress and purpose
Can our Congress express?

Other than to grandstand, stalemate, point fingers and
blame.
Rather than generate favorable press
They just continue their mess
It's time for job descriptions
And yearly performance evaluations.

Congress should not be a circus
Of animal clowns primarily Elephants and Donkeys
Filling their coffers to get re-elected
Promising solutions that never get enacted.

Too much time wasted on procedural process
The heart and soul of mindless congress
Efficiency and effectiveness has to become their intent
To focus on bills that have meaningful content.

Elevate your personal behavior
Aim to be our savior
Rise above the rest
America expects your best!

A NATURAL PROGRESSION

Babies have to cry and crawl
Toddlers have to fall
To play and have fun
Enjoying nature, toys, and sun.

Children should evolve into adolescents
When they're in their teens
But now it's forced on the "in-betweens"
Little time to distinguish ends from means.

Experiencing life's school lessons
Takes a natural steady pace
Not meant to be a race
Values clarification needs space.

Human maturation is a crucial process
To reach full developmental readiness
But our media's messages are a mess
Promoting instant age compressed happiness.

SPORTS

SUNFISHING

Make ready first
Then thigh high
Shove off
Pull in, trim

Glide, swift
Banging wet
Coming about
Again and again

Boat and sailor
Together one
With the changing
Fickle wind

Feeling, looking
Reading, guessing
All the time
Nature's clues

Which air and
Water make
Visible
If you look

GOLF – A FOUR-LETTER WORD

Where is the Scotsman
That invented Golf
The ultimate four-letter word
What was he thinking or drinking?

The courses are green and nice
With an expensive price
But why the sand, rough,
And all the water?

I bought the latest hi-tech clubs,
Waterproof shoes and gloves
Took lessons, read books.
Only to shoot the same hooks.

I keep looking for birdies and eagles
But haven't found any yet
I'll celebrate a par
In the nearest bar!

FISHIN' A WAY OF LIFE

Still have the fascination
Stay awake all night anticipation
From that first time experience fishing
Now has become a passionate mission

A reason to be outdoors, to relax
With no cell phone or fax
Must stay on red alert
For that subtle bite and fight

Let the fish be feeding
And I do no weeding
May the white caps be down
Cause I don't want to drown

So set the drag, keep a tight line
You'll do just fine
Sharpen your hook
For something to cook

I pray this old party boat
Will stay afloat
And the captain imposes a fine
On anyone who snags my line

Oh, what a sport, enjoying nature
With friends, perhaps with a wager,
Swapping stories that change
Like the weight of that bass, with age.

When the clock says it's time
To be back at the dock
May the cooler fit
Our limit

But if excuses you need
From this list you can read
Wrong tide, dirty tide, red tide,
And the best, wind against tide

And on my last day, God,
I don't want a band
Please, let me be on the water
With a rod in my hand

THE RAPTURE OF DEER HUNTING

It's the preparation
So much anticipation
Find the best location
For tomorrow's hopeful celebration.

Get the long Johns ready
Set the alarm clock early
Pray for a little snow, cold and bright
For tracking and better sight

Now it's time to lock and load
Ready for whatever will unfold
Senses focused with all your might
Checking out every sound and sight

Look hard for signs of a deer
For they surely will appear
Stay alert and ready
Remember to keep your aim steady

Look there's one, no two!
Control the buck fever, I must do
To squeeze the trigger
With this unsteady finger

FEELINGS

WHAT I'D GIVE TO SHARE THIS FEELING!

What I'd give-to play a clarinet
Soft, romantic, jazz, clairvoyant

Or paint a picture to be framed
Proud, crisp, true, unique

Oh, to write a poem that could stand by itself,
Precise, concise, complete

Or anyway to express what's building up inside
To give it form so you and I can share it!

SELF PERCEPTION

Why do I hate myself
So easily so, freely?
How bad was my blunder
To hear so much inner thunder

I cannot flip
Or take a trip
My greatest deception
Is my own self-perception

THANKS, BEST FRIENDS

Learn to accept, trust, and depend
On loving yourself, becoming your own best friend
A friend to value and hold on to tight
All through life's long flight.

Remaining strong, absorbing pain
Not expecting daily gain
But flexible, tolerant, faithful
An attitude of gratitude.

Yet, when you feel it's hard to mend
Communicate with your external best friend
Who will understand your fears
Share, and dry your tears.

For sometimes we need both for survival
Preventing the if in life, being a conquering rival
Together, we, me and you
Will make it through.

<u>TRUE LOVE IS</u>

<u>AN EVERLASTING ICE CREAM CONE OF...</u>

Acceptance of who you are
A word put into action...a verb
Magical, mysterious, marvelous
Will and discipline combined
Unconditional acceptance
Buoyant force – Supportive
Silent understanding
Compatible values
Values differences
Unselfish devotion
Transcends reality
Encouragement
An equilibrium
True friendship
Affectionate
Tenderness
Passionate
Synergistic
Optimistic
Forgiving
Sensitive
Intimate
Respect
Hopeful
Patient
Honest
Loyal
Trust
Joy
US

<u>FALLING IN LOVE IS EASY,</u>
<u>STAYING IN LOVE IS HARD</u>

Falling in love was easy
There was affection, acceptance
Laughter, admiration
Intimacy, emotion
Reciprocal devotion

We listened to each other
Felt light as a feather
Our relationship was effortless
Yet, over time,
Where are we now?

Romance, so strong
Seems to be gone
We're not sharing
Or even caring
Only experiencing disappointments

Egos originally separate
Fused into one
Returning to two again
Disillusioned, hurt
Ready to fight

For us to truly mend
We need to be a friend
I can't do us alone
We need to work together
To love us again, anew

MUSIC – MY PASSION

While we are always hearing,
Seldom are we really listening
'Cause we didn't place the receiver between the lines
Pleasant, desired sounds are hard to find

Reliable, like peak fall foliage to enjoy
Or, a steady waterfall cascading down
Heightening deep feelings of peace and joy
Music, is a special free adult toy

Sensory perfection is hard to find
Yet, any symphony is absolutely divine
Or, a soulful melody enhanced with perfect lyrics that
magically blend
So I can again look forward to visiting my loyal friend

The sound of music
So fluid and Dynamic
A continuous charge
That creates a mirage

FEELING DOWN?

At times, we all feel down
Yet, there's no reason to frown
What we need to find
Is the constant smile on our mind

Understand how you're feeling
Is what you're thinking
Re-frame your mental picture, be your best friend
Always ready to help you mend

<u>ENOUGH IS ENOUGH!</u>

Why did it take us so long to get this low?
Not understanding our negative downward flow
Bringing us to a state of deep despair
Even with all I've invested, I now really don't care

Loss of importance, pride, expectation, and desire
Have all put out my heart's fire
Any attempts to try to go back
End by your continuous verbal attack

Bottoming out takes a long time
Rationalizations rampant in my mind
Obligations and myths about my role
Ultimately take their heavy toll

Shakespeare tells us that readiness and ripeness is all
He's right, but did I endure the long fall?
Because I wasn't ready and ripe
Able to muster my courage and might

It took the slow process of super saturation
To finally create my need for salvation
Now, instead of staying in the heat
I'm moving on by standing on my own two feet

SPIRITUAL – PHILOSOPHICAL

MEANING OF LIFE

What is the meaning of life
Who do I ask?
Life is an unpredictable force
That affects us all differently

Life is what happens
When we've planned something else
Only you can find, adapt and create
To adjust and make the most from fate

That's why *if* is in life
External life is obscure, unfeeling
Its meaning becomes evident, though, … if
We do some introspection and reflection

ALCHEMY

What's wrong with
Making something into
What it's not?

We're not base metal
Really gold
When made such

By the magic
Of expectation
And a loving touch

PARADOX

So much is
Really upside down
Inside out
Wet-dry, elusive
Look hard for
The real message
In the sunrise
And you'll find it
In the sunset

MOODS

Without the range
From freezing to boiling
Mountain top
To valley low
Life's steps go nowhere
Like impressions in
Wave swept sand

AFTER ELEVEN

Sunlight fills everywhere
Like darkness
Enveloping
Overtaking

Both penetrate
Pressing us
Saying senses – feel
What's in is out

Cosmic energy shared
In day, receiving, seeing
At night looking up
Sending back, Knowing

For the morning
We're more aware of earth
After Eleven
We're in Heaven

DREAM CATCHERS

To enrich our existence, we dream
Passive, waiting for sleep, but
We need to look inside, deep
To find our secret stream

It runs through us constantly
Searching for a river to empty into
To flow further, no matter how far
To become who we know we really are

Is your dream catcher
Wise words from your father?
The wishes of your mother?
Or your own inner drummer?

To catch your message
Continue on the passage
Filtering that confusion
Doing away with illusion

Our heart and soul
Combine to know
What our mind
Alone cannot find

HEARTS' SONG

Burning with hidden desire
Is our hearts fire
Increasing our vision
Of life's mission

To find our heart's core voice
We must make the choice
To listen, To be devoured
So we become empowered.

By lyrics, pure, exceptional
Secret, unique, vital
Created by our heart and mind.
So our soul we find.

AMEN

Hope springs forth
From, the ground below
Flowing into branches high
It's Easter!

God's eternal energy
Expressed to us in hope...
By his risen Son
And in a tulip bed

Hope to understand
That rebirth is constant
Hope that redefines a necessary transformation
We greet cheerlessly – and call death

Hope that helps us say
To life,
To death,
Amen

<u>PEACE AND WAR</u>

Why is peace
So out of reach?
Desired, wished, prayed for
Yet, behind a mind-locked door.

War seems more welcome
Easier to kill than love
History, hate and anger
Generate more emotional power

Peace is difficult to achieve
Requiring heart, mind and soul to believe
Commitment, faith, hope and transcendence
Elevating to a higher level of consciousness

Afterword

To be nobody, but myself in a world which is doing its best night and day to make you everybody else, means to fight the hardest battle which any human can fight, and never stop fighting.

- e.e. cummings

The whole of life lies in the verb seeing.

- Pierre Teilard De Chardin

Follow your instincts: that's where true wisdom manifests itself.

- Oprah Winfrey

After my writings, I did some deep introspection on why and what made me stay dedicated to this task. First, my memory is full of experiences that shaped my worldview. They remain vivid and easily recalled. I feel some had such a profound effect on me. I share with you my challenging choices that were empowered by maintaining and applying an optimistic attitude to my life. Although some were unpleasant, they all helped me gain self-confidence and courage to fulfill my potential.

I am also aware of the adaptations required by life. Changes in values, technology, communication, education, culture, quality of life, economics, etc. have influenced my philosophy of life. We have to constantly look for, and find, the "silver linings" to function in an ever-changing world.

This process of constant adaptation and change requires internal growth. I had to overcome obstacles through maintaining my self-respect and inner pride. This process was primarily done by accepting challenging choices and acting on them. Positive self-esteem is a by-product of what you accomplish. We develop our personal treasures by discovering and tackling life's problems and challenges. We can't do much about the <u>quantity</u> of our life. What we can do, is live a profound <u>quality</u> of life; by applying passion, positive attitude, faith, and soul, to co-create love and appreciation for ourselves, loved ones, friends, others, and nature, every minute of every day.

With Judy, her acceptance and respect, I was able to regain a feeling of being whole and reborn. My enthusiasm and energy returned and brought me new life. These awakened feelings drew me to write poetry about emotions of joy, and my appreciation of life.

Challenging choices provide us with opportunities for continuous enrichment. Let the following thoughts provide direction to the wind beneath your wings, on your journey through the mystery, magic, music, marvel, and miracle of your life.

What is right for one soul may not be right for another. It may mean having to stand on your own and do something strange in the eyes of others.

- Eileen Caddy

Making choices is the most powerful thing that you do in your life. Choices liberate, and they imprison. They create illness, and they create health, they shape your life. Each choice creates a future.

- Gary Zukov

Keep a clear eye toward life's end. Do not forget your purpose and destiny as God's creature. What you are in his sight is what you are and nothing more. Remember that when you leave this earth, you can take nothing that you have received,... but only what you have given; a full heart enriched by honest service, love, sacrifice, and courage.

- St. Francis of Assisi

Bon Voyage,

Cliff

About the Author

For thirty-two years, Clifford Bennett served in two Long Island pubic school systems as; the director of student support services, special and health education, middle school principal, high school assistant principal, science department chairperson, teacher of science, and coach. He received his professional diploma from Queens College (CUNY), and his master's and bachelor's degrees from Hofstra University. Cliff served as an adjunct instructor at Hofstra University from 1961 to 1969, and was an adjunct assistant professor of education and field supervisor of student teachers at Dowling College for ten years after his retirement from public education in 1991.

He has presented workshops at national, state, and local levels on prevention of self-defeating behaviors, stress management and personal growth, wellness-holistic health, and dynamics of self-esteem. He has published twenty-seven articles on educational and mental health issues in numerous professional journals.

He is father of four children and grandfather of eight. He resides in Holbrook, New York, and Estero, Florida, with his wife, Judy. His hobbies include all outdoor activities, especially, gardening, fishing, golf, as well as reading, and writing poetry.